Nordic-Baltic-American Cooperation

Shaping the U.S.–European Agenda

Edited by
Kurt Volker and Ieva Kupce

Center for Transatlantic Relations
Paul H. Nitze School of Advanced International Studies
Johns Hopkins University

Kurt Volker and Ieva Kupce, *Nordic-Baltic-American Cooperation: Shaping the U.S.-European Agenda*

Washington, DC: Center for Transatlantic Relations, 2012.

Center for Transatlantic Relations
The Paul H. Nitze School of Advanced International Studies
The Johns Hopkins University
1717 Massachusetts Ave., NW, Suite 525
Washington, DC 20036
Tel: (202) 663-5880
Fax (202) 663-5879
Email: transatlantic@jhu.edu
http://transatlantic.sais-jhu.edu

ISBN 978-0-9848544-7-9

Cover illustration: Norwegian Sea, near Bodø, Norway, by Kurt Volker.

Table of Contents

Introduction

Kurt Volker

When one hears about the transatlantic relationship these days, one usually hears about some form of crisis. The Euro crisis. The debt crisis. Individual nations' financial crises. The future-of-NATO crisis, including the crisis in defense spending. The continuing crisis in Afghanistan. How to handle the Syria crisis... the list seems to never end.

But the Nordic-Baltic region is not in crisis. Here is a region that is stable, prosperous, financially sound, growing economically, and... peaceful. The nations in this region are members of the EU, or NATO, or in some cases both. It is a region that has managed its own affairs, and has an outlook on the affairs of the world.

It is a region from which we might take a lesson or two.

First, it is proof positive that market democracy is not a failing system. Yes, the United States, the EU/Euro-zone, and individual Euro-members such as Spain and Greece are finding it difficult, if not impossible, to make sound fiscal decisions. But the Nordic-Baltic region is proving that the problem is not with market democracy itself, but with the decision-making of individuals and individual states. Authoritarian capitalism in China, Islamism in many countries, or neo-mercantilism in Brazil or India may give a sense of short-term appeal. But in the long run, they have nothing on that powerful combination of freedom, democracy, human rights, the rule of law, and free markets.

Kurt Volker is a former U.S. Ambassador to NATO and Senior Fellow at the Center for Transatlantic Relations at the Paul H. Nitze School of Advanced International Studies (SAIS) at Johns Hopkins University.

Second, the Nordic-Baltic region is a reminder that the democratic market-based economies of the world have something to say about a positive outward vision of the world. They remind us that we are capable of—and have a direct interest in—strengthening respect for universal human values and building greater international cooperation and global security.

Third, they remind us that the work of the transatlantic community through its key institutions—the European Union, NATO, and the OSCE—is far from over.

This book is intended to flesh out exactly what kind of vision the Nordic-Baltic states—together with the United States—can bring to the transatlantic table. It follows on an earlier project by the Atlantic Council of the United States, and—with the generous support of the Foreign Ministries of Sweden, Lithuania and Latvia—aims to take that work another step forward.

The Nordic-Baltic states have something to offer in dozens of areas—from sound fiscal policies to population-growth policies to environmental management. For the purposes of this project—and looking in particular at how to contribute to the NATO and EU agendas—we have selected five areas to review:

- First is the continued promotion of a Europe whole, free, and at peace. As difficult as it is now for NATO and the EU to manage the many crises afflicting the transatlantic area—first and foremost our budget crises—the fact remains that NATO and EU enlargement has been one of the most important success stories of the past century. Over 100 million people in the Euro-Atlantic area now live in freedom, democracy, relative prosperity, and fundamental security, compared to just 25 years ago. The Nordic-Baltic states retain this vision about the continued spread of freedom and democracy throughout all of Europe, and can help reignite the drive for such a spread within NATO and the EU themselves.

- Second is the issue of regional integration, or "embedding." The Nordic-Baltic states have found ways to produce higher political and security value through closer integration than they could possibly produce as a disparate collection of individual states and policies. At a time when NATO and EU solidarity is facing unprecedented challenges, the lesson of successful integration and "embedding" is a powerful one.

- Third is the relationship with Russia. The United States, Western Europe, and Central and Eastern Europe have at least three or four different policies toward Russia—at a time when Russia itself is becoming more authoritarian at home, and assertive in what it calls its "near abroad." The Nordic-Baltic states border Russia, and as such have a direct interest and valuable perspective on living with Russia as a neighbor—everything from managing security and environmental issues to seeing the linkages between Russia's authoritarian system and its external behavior. The Nordic-Baltic states cannot change Russia on their own—but they can contribute to building a more coherent EU and NATO policy toward Russia.

- Fourth—and closely tied to the issue of managing relations with Russia—is the issue of energy security. The Nordic-Baltic states—as immediate neighbors of Russia—stand out again as models for managing the complicated issues involving energy security today. We see in Sweden and Denmark, for example, impressive policies for reducing energy demand while preserving high economic output and quality of life. In Norway, we see production of massive amounts of oil and natural gas. In Finland and Lithuania we see expansion of nuclear power production. In Estonia we have a decades-old model for exploiting the "new" fuel of shale-energy production. There remains high dependence on Russia in some states, such as Lithuania and Latvia. But at the same time, there is also a concerted effort by all states in the region to move toward greater energy sustainability—a policy model worth examining in both the EU and NATO.

- Finally, there is the relationship with the United States. At a time when one hears talk of a "pivot" to Asia and "leading from behind"—and one observes major U.S. troop withdrawals from Europe—the question arises: How can one keep the United States engaged in Europe? The experience of the recent past, a weak European security capacity depending on major U.S. engagement, has proven unsustainable. America will not make up for the gap in European defense capability indefinitely. And nor will America—vulnerable as it is to the European debt crisis—step in to bail out Europe, when Europe is lacking the political will, more than it lacks wealth, to solve its own problems.

The Nordic-Baltic states offer yet again an interesting model of retaining U.S. engagement—by becoming net contributors to wealth, foreign policy management, development assistance and security, rather than remaining net consumers. Sweden, a non-ally, took part in NATO's Libya operation and still plays a major role in Afghanistan. Norway and Denmark were Alliance leaders in airstrikes in Libya. Lithuania, Latvia and Estonia each stepped up to contribute to Afghanistan, showing a commitment to the Alliance a whole, even though their resources are small. This is important because the Nordic-Baltic region still depends upon active U.S. engagement—from the Joint Strike Fighter partnership with Norway, to major exercises and air policing in the Baltic States. While there can be no guarantee of security in the Nordic-Baltic region without the United States, there is also no sustainability to such a U.S. role without substantial contributions from the Nordic-Baltic states themselves. Once again, the Nordic-Baltic region offers a model for Europe and NATO as whole, where U.S. engagement remains paramount, yet is diminishing under political and budgetary pressures.

Clearly, there are differences within the Nordic-Baltic region, and even great differences between this region and the rest of Europe. But by taking a close look at the successes of the region in these critical areas, we can perhaps draw some useful lessons on strengthening NATO and the European Union writ large, and in inspiring a more positive, outward-looking perspective amid the gloom that surrounds transatlantic discussions at the moment.

Executive Summary

Per Augustsson, Erik Brattberg

The broader transatlantic relationship is increasingly described in terms of crisis. The European Union as a whole is focused on financial crisis management. And there is disappointment in Washington over Europe's inability to step up as a more serious security partner.

Meanwhile, the Nordic-Baltic region stands out as a stable, responsible and dynamic part of Europe. As net contributors to prosperity, foreign policy management, development assistance and security, the region shows that market democracy still works, that a positive outward vision of the world is still possible and that there is still important work ahead for the transatlantic institutions. In fact, the region offers a model of how to retain U.S. engagement in Europe.

So, what kind of vision can the Nordic-Baltic countries—together with the United States—bring today to the transatlantic table? How can the Nordic-Baltic countries and the U.S. cooperate to shape the broader transatlantic agenda in a positive direction?

The CTR project on Nordic-Baltic-American cooperation follows on an earlier project by the Atlantic Council of the United States. With generous support from the Foreign Ministries of Sweden, Lithuania and Latvia, it aims to explore which concrete contributions can be made—in particular to the EU and NATO agendas—in five areas:

- The continued promotion of a Europe whole, free and at peace
- Regional integration or "embedding"
- The relationship with Russia
- Energy security
- U.S. engagement with Europe

In the run-up to the NATO summit in Chicago, a number of leading scholars and practitioners from the United States and Europe have contributed with their ideas and recommendations. Their findings can be summarized as follows:

Europe Whole and Free

- Europe is not yet unified and free. Principles of political pluralism, free markets, the rule of law, media freedom and respect for human rights are not adhered to by everyone. *Much work remains.*

- The transatlantic bond is weakening. The European unwillingness to take more responsibility in the area of defense and security is undermining its position in the U.S. NATO and the EU remain the key institutions for security and prosperity in Europe but the *effectiveness of policies depend on unity.*

- The Euro-Atlantic institutions must be proactive in managing transformations. They must be able to respond to new conditions and requirements in order to be successful. A *holistic approach* is needed to security, encompassing not only political and military dimensions but also for example economics and information technology.

- The lack of trust between EU/NATO countries and Russia is a major problem. Concrete action to *promote trust and cooperation* between Russia and its neighbors and between Russia and NATO could be taken in the areas of conflict resolution, military confidence-building, information-sharing, joint exercises and reconciliation (for example as proposed in the EASI Final Report of 2012).

- In the context of the financial and economic crisis, perceptions of an East/West divide within the EU are partly misleading. The Baltic countries—as the Nordics, but unlike some older EU members—have shown willingness to reform. In terms of sound financial choices, the Nordic-Baltic EU members have more in common than the Euro-zone overall.

New EU members should be at the forefront in the debate about European responsibility and solidarity.

Embedding and Integration

- There is a global trend towards more common international military action, as opposed to individual national action. The future will most likely see further military integration. In a European context, *financial realities* will speed up integration, including in the area of defense industries.

- The Afghanistan operation has resulted in generally increased levels of integration of militaries. But the operations in Afghanistan and Libya have also illustrated that many problems remain regarding *capabilities*.

- The Nordic-Baltic countries seem to recognize that they are all *dependent on each other's security*. At the same time, sensitivities remain concerning practical expressions of military solidarity. The reluctance of Sweden and Finland to join NATO effectively obstructs the practical ability of the Nordic-Baltic region to form a true security community. If defense planning of all the eight countries would be performed within a NATO framework, the Nordic-Baltic countries would be brought even closer together and military threats to the region would diminish considerably. The freedom of maneuver for any aggressor would be extremely limited.

- The Nordic-Baltic region has nevertheless reached a relatively *advanced stage of defense integration*. The cooperation has been pragmatic. NORDEFCO provides a mutually beneficial process and a practical way of training for military interoperability. Swedish and Finnish involvement in NATO and U.S.-led Baltic security increases regional security. A further test will be the ability to deliver common procurement programs. Consistent, rather than sporadic, multinational procurement is one of the real tests of deep integration.

- The Nordic-Baltic process can bring *added value to European security*. The region will probably see more of integrated education, Baltic Sea maritime cooperation and a greater joint ability to field larger integrated units. The integration process should be further deepened and broadened to include more of Northern Europe and NATO. Further deepening and broadening should cover lessons learned from Afghanistan, cyber defense and the High North.

• Cooperation on *non-military security* is also important in areas such as crisis management, energy infrastructure, the fight against organized crime, border security and illegal migration.

• The U.S. must maintain the reassurance that NORDEFCO complements—rather than supplements—the U.S. role in the Baltic. US-Nordic-Baltic cooperation could expand to include maritime surveillance, procurement, intelligence and counter-intelligence. *The U.S. should get further involved* in joint exercises, financial support, in providing excess defense articles and through rotational training deployments. The Baltic region must be part of an irreducible U.S. military commitment to Europe. The exercise "Steadfast Jazz" in October-November 2013 should be made a serious one.

• Further U.S. engagement would send a message of recognition of the regional efforts and of the fact that the efforts have improved security arrangements for *the benefit of the U.S. and NATO*. It would also enhance U.S. capabilities and tighten the bond between the U.S. and Northern European allies.

• The financial and economic crisis and the current budget austerity present an opportunity to remove obstacles to cooperation. However, *military cooperation is not easy*. It requires adaptation, reliance on others and—sometimes—a more complicated decision-making process.

• Experiences show that successful military cooperation requires a *culture of cooperation* not only among policy makers but also at the level of people who have to deliver the practical cooperation. It requires compatibility with regard to military education systems. Joint military educational establishments have far-reaching impact on the cooperation potential. Educational exchange programs are also helpful. Another crucial factor is the ability to communicate in the same language at all levels in the organization. English is used among the Nordic-Baltic countries.

- *Long-term perspectives* are needed for successful cooperation. In order for integration to work, countries must be prepared to politically accept giving up certain industrial interests, accept limits to national sovereign decision-making and withstand various national political pressures. It must also be clearly demonstrated that cooperation leads to better practical results and larger benefits than national solutions.

Russia and the East

- In theory, US/EU goals for Eastern Europe regarding self-determination, economic development and freedom do not clash with Russia's vision. And Russia and the West share interests in stemming drug trade and terrorism. However, in practice, the two sides offer *very different societal models* to Eastern Europe.

- The financial and economic crisis has made the West less attractive. This makes the work more difficult. At the same time, EU and NATO countries are increasingly unanimous in their analyses of Russia. In addition, Russian society has overcome its political apathy. This means that *conditions for a serious debate on Russia have improved.* Such a debate should include historians, academics and business people.

- The Russo-Western dialogue should include a conversation about *common interests* in the neighborhood. Pragmatic opportunities for cooperation should be used on issues such as the security of Afghanistan after NATO's withdrawal.

- Even if the West's ability to directly influence Russia's strategic direction is limited, there are important *concrete measures* that can be taken in several areas in the broader Eastern European neighborhood.

- The *EU's Eastern Partnership*, which promises partner countries close cooperation and integration based on conditionality, is of major importance. It should be further developed in areas such as youth exchange, culture, scholarships for students, twinning programs, civil society support, exchange of best practices, support for small and medium-sized businesses, visa-facilities and anti-corruption efforts. Transatlantic coordination and support from the U.S. in this work could be of great importance.

• There is *no one-size-fits-all* with regard to the Partner countries. Financial support should be considered on the basis of needs and achievements. Energy resources and exports should affect the needs assessments. Partner countries that have reached agreement with the EU on a Deep and Comprehensive Free Trade Area should be given help in preparing themselves for future entry into the EU internal market.

• Partner countries should be brought into the framework of the *EU's Common Security and Defense Policy.* Their participation in crisis management operations could foster dialogue and promote reforms. Programs like the Erasmus for militaries and diplomats in EU institutions should be open to partner countries. Partner countries should also be invited to participate in the EU battle groups in order to promote reform and confidence building.

• *Energy reform* should be a priority in Eastern Europe. Dependence on Russia and lack of transparency are major problems. The Ukraine and Moldova have joined the European "Energy Community" and the EU should hold them to their obligations and be ready to support reforms with money and expertise.

• *The U.S.-Nordic-Baltic group is a good fit* in dealing with the promotion of security and freedom in the East. The countries of the group are outward looking, economically vigorous and their diversity is useful. Their proximity to Russia concentrates minds and their shared values are particularly important at a time when broader transatlantic cooperation seems to be weakening. U.S.-Nordic-Baltic efforts in relation to Russia and the East should not exclude others. The Visegrad countries and the U.K could also be valuable partners in the work.

- Reaching out to *Russian civil society* will be important for the West in the coming years. Informal donor conferences could be organized by the U.S. and the Nordic-Baltic countries and assistance could be offered. Assistance should not only be directed to NGOs but also to schools, health care institutions and environmental organizations. The U.S. and the Nordic-Baltic countries could develop and fund initiatives for foreign policy debate. The embassies could also organize informal meetings with Russian journalists and bloggers in order to break through the propaganda filter. Social media could be used more.

- Russian *propaganda* against the Baltic States should be condemned. The U.S. and the Nordic-Baltic countries should counter propaganda by holding Russia responsible for its words and by following up on statements.

- The US-Nordic-Baltic group should implement *"the Magnitsky list"* visa sanctions in relation to Russia and instigate money laundering investigations against people who have enriched themselves through bribe-taking and theft.

- The West should engage in *Belarus' transformation*, not isolation. A weak and isolated Belarus is easy prey for Moscow. There should be a focus on interaction with ordinary people, expanding business and human links. The US-Nordic-Baltic group should target Belarus with sanctions at the top and at the same time assist in areas such as visas, legal aid and the media. The EU visa ban should be kept on those responsible for the fate of political prisoners. Visa costs for ordinary Belarusians should be removed or lowered to a minimum.

Energy Security

- Natural gas plays a more strategic role in Europe today than any other fuel. However, the European natural gas market suffers from *several structural deficiencies*. One of the main challenges to Europe's energy security comes from Russia. Russian political leaders have, at times, exploited European fears of gas cut-offs in order to strengthen Gazprom's monopolistic power.

- The differences in size, location and background between Germany, Poland and the Baltic countries have contributed to *policy differences*. National energy mixes, perceptions and strategies vary considerably due to domestic energy production, established supply routes, infrastructure and political preferences. As a result, the Baltic countries (and partly Finland) constitute an "energy island" with one company (Gazprom) as the region's predominant gas supplier. The launch of the Nord Stream gas pipeline in November 2011 also raised concerns in the region regarding security of supply and the liberalization of energy markets.

- The European Union has been working for over a decade with the formation of a unified internal energy market by 2014. Europe seeks to maximize its energy security through hub-based trading, since *efficient markets maximize security of supply* at fair prices without political interference. Despite regional energy initiatives, a comprehensive and effective regional energy architecture or institutional framework is still absent in the Baltic region.

- *The Nordic-Baltic countries can play a significant role* by catalyzing the development of a more liquid natural gas market in Europe and by eliminating so-called "energy islands" in the Baltic region. Facilitating the eastward spread of market-based gas trading into the Baltic Basin is the most significant step that can be taken to strengthen Europe's energy security with respect to natural gas.

- The Nordic-Baltic countries are currently taking steps towards a regional energy security strategy that supports the EU's goals of a liberalized natural gas market and integrated electricity grids among all its members. But, they are not integrating these measures into a joint, coordinated plan. The Nordic-Baltic countries should therefore, together with Poland, seek to develop a *joint Baltic Basin Energy Market Strategy*, which would define a vision for the emergence of natural gas trading hubs and integrated electricity grids among the Baltic Basin and Nordic countries, Poland, and other EU partners.

- The Nordic-Baltic countries should also promote a more transparent and market-based *Ukrainian behavior* regarding natural gas transit, as well as a more market-based behavior from *Gazprom*, including more constructive relations with European consumers, Caspian exporters and independent Russian gas producers.

- The transatlantic dimension in the energy security agenda of the Baltic region has been somewhat secondary. The most pressing energy challenges in the Baltic Sea region—natural gas supplies and liberalization—have been regional and European rather than transatlantic issues. U.S. involvement has been largely limited to regional energy diplomacy. However, some precursors exist for a more enhanced transatlantic relationship in regional energy security developments. The EU-U.S. Energy Council in 2009 provided an indication of the *mutual understanding needed* for a stronger institutional interaction between the two transatlantic counterparts.

U.S. Engagement

- A strong transatlantic link remains indispensable for enhancing common values and interest within the Euro-Atlantic area and beyond. Although there are differences between the U.S. and Europe, and growing American weariness over Europe's inability to assume greater strategic responsibilities, the common values and principles underpinning the transatlantic relationship remain relevant. In fact, in today's world, the *U.S. needs Europe as much as Europe needs the U.S.*

- The EU's Common European Security and Defence Policy is still in the making but better integration of military forces/structures and rationalizing European procurement remain key European objectives. The recent Libya operation demonstrated the importance of transatlantic cooperation and *reinforced the European pillar* of the transatlantic link.

- NATO's partnership policy is one of NATO's main strengths and added values. By opening the doors to both regional and global partnerships, NATO is *strengthening its overall legitimacy* as a global security provider. This is important not only in the context of troop contributions to NATO-led operations but also in enabling partners to provide support and active cooperation regarding common threats and security challenges.

- *The Nordic-Baltic region offers many assets* to the transatlantic community. They are leaders in the effort to promote democracy, rule of law, human rights, and market-based development in Europe and around the world. They are also regarded as "honest brokers" in many of the world's hotspots. Moreover, the Nordic-Baltic region has steadfastly supported the vision of a Europe whole, free, undivided, and secure.

- Taken together, the Nordic-Baltic region offers some significant useable, deployable military assets. The willingness to support NATO missions goes beyond the NATO members and also includes non-members Finland and Sweden. Their assets make them a *compelling partner* for the United States.

- A U.S.-Nordic-Baltic agenda can leverage these attributes to address regional and global developments affecting the transatlantic community. The agenda could include revitalizing the vision of a *Europe Whole, Free, and Secure*, making *Arctic security* a priority in U.S.-Nordic-Baltic engagement, pursuing a coordinated engagement with *Russia*, leveraging Nordic-Baltic Capacities for *Out of Area Operations*, and deepening U.S.-Nordic-Baltic *military engagement*.

Chapter One

What Makes the Nordic-Baltic Region So Interesting to the U.S.?

Per Augustsson and Erik Brattberg

Why should the U.S. work even more closely with the countries of the Nordic-Baltic region? And why should the countries of the Nordic-Baltic region look for ways to strengthen their regional cooperation even further?

A U.S.–Nordic-Baltic Opportunity

Global power is shifting from the West to the East. Asia is ascendant, while Europe and the U.S. struggle with economic recovery, political polarization and low self-confidence. And while the transatlantic partnership is still the strongest economic and political intercontinental relationship in the world, it needs attention and political energy in order to continue to flourish and develop. Commitment to a concrete agenda of further cooperation is needed from strong and confident partners on both sides of the Atlantic. This agenda includes global issues but also issues pertaining specifically to Europe, such as prosperity and stability in Eastern and Southeastern Europe, cooperation with Russia, energy security, strategies for the High North and pragmatic security cooperation in times of austerity. Indeed, as the world undergoes transformation and power shifts, the need for transatlantic cooperation on all these issues may be more important than ever.

Current dynamics, however, seem to be working in other directions. Europe's financial and economic crisis has forced European leaders to

Per Augustsson and Erik Brattberg are, respectively, a Senior Fellow and a Visiting Fellow at the Center for Transatlantic Relations at the Paul H. Nitze School of Advanced International Studies (SAIS) at Johns Hopkins University.

devote most of their political energy towards internal crisis management rather than on the strategic external agenda. Meanwhile, America's urgent attention is needed elsewhere in the world and its patience seems to be running low with Europe's real or perceived inability to come together as one and step up as a more serious security partner. As a result, the transatlantic agenda and the development of joint policies on European neighborhood issues risk being put on the backburner. This potential vacuum and the multiplicity of current challenges present a situation where new avenues of collaboration could be explored in trying to make progress on concrete issues related to transatlantic security. Here, the Nordic-Baltic region—which already cooperates closely with the U.S., for example through the e-PINE framework—has the opportunity to play an even more instrumental role in serving as a key European partner to the U.S. on a number of issues, both in and beyond Europe. And the Nordic-Baltic region is a particularly attractive partner to the U.S. for a host of reasons.

A Region Gaining in Relevance

Increasing Geostrategic Importance

The Nordic-Baltic region of Northern Europe, comprising Denmark, Estonia, Finland, Iceland, Latvia, Lithuania, Norway, and Sweden, is located on roughly the same latitude as Alaska, the largest state of the United States. Compared to Alaska, however, the Nordic-Baltic region (including Greenland) is more than double its size and home to 45 times more people. Even excluding Greenland, the Nordic-Baltic region is larger in size than Germany, France, and Italy put together.[1] The region's sea areas are vast, with territorial waters and exclusive economic zones comparable to those of the whole European Union.[2]

The region, in particular through Norway and Greenland (which is a part of Denmark), is Europe's face towards the High North and the Arctic Sea, an area with increasing geopolitical importance in terms of resources, global shipping, maritime safety and international cooperation. Energy production in the Nordic-Baltic region is equal to

---

[1] Nordic Statistical Yearbook, p. 22.

[2] Eurocean, PEW, Wikipedia.

36 percent of the EU's total production.[3] Here, Norway stands out in the region as Western Europe's single biggest oil producer. Most of the European Union's direct border with Russia is through the Nordic-Baltic region and close to 40 percent of Russia's total border with different European countries is represented by the Nordic-Baltic region.[4] The region can also be seen as an East–West bridge, both in terms of the Nordic-Baltic dimension itself and through its engagement in the wider Eastern European neighborhood.

A History of Pragmatic Cooperation

There are many differences between the individual countries of the Nordic-Baltic region in terms of geography, historical experiences, and security political orientations. Some of them are members of NATO, some of them are members of the EU, and some of them are members of both. In spite of differences, they share many interests and a tradition of working together through a number of regional forums and organizations. The countries of the Nordic region have cooperated longer and deeper than most other countries and regions in the world. And since the end of the Cold War, this regional cooperation has extended to the Baltic countries. The increasingly close contacts cover many sectors and levels of society, and are based on trust, pragmatism, and shared values and interests (more on this below). And the combination of differences and shared interests make the dynamics particularly interesting.

More recently, the region has also strengthened its strategic dialogue (primarily on economic and social issues) with the United Kingdom through the so-called Northern Future Forum, where the heads of government of the eight Nordic-Baltic countries and the UK participate. With regard to the Arctic, the Nordic countries are engaged in dialogue and cooperation with Canada, Russia, and the U.S. within the framework of the Arctic Council.

---

[3] OECD Factbook 2011 (Latvia and Lithuania are not included here nor in any of the other OECD Factbook data cited below).

[4] Geography.about.com, a part of the New York Times Company.

A Stable and Responsible Region

The Nordic-Baltic region is one of the most stable regions in the world. Four of the region's countries find themselves on the top ten list of the Global Peace Index,[5] and only a small number of latent issues in the region are registered by the Conflict Barometer,[6] for example the Russian-speaking minorities in Estonia and Latvia and the Danish–Canadian disagreement about the ownership of Hans Island just west of Greenland. Compared to other European countries, only five (the UK, France, Russia, Germany, and Italy) spend more on defense than the Nordic-Baltic region taken as a whole.[7] Regional defense collaboration is far-reaching. The Nordic Defence Cooperation platform (NORDEFCO), which promotes synergies and effective common defense solutions, has recently also undertaken efforts to enhance dialogue with the three Baltic states. The region has contributed responsibly to international military missions, including in Afghanistan and the Balkans, and to the EU's Nordic Battle Group (see below). Also, in terms of perceived corruption, four of the region's countries rank among the top ten least corrupt in the world.[8]

A Part of Europe with Economic Growth

The Nordic-Baltic region is in better economic shape than other parts of Europe. On average, the Nordic-Baltic economies are predicted to grow by about two percent in 2012, compared to zero growth for the EU as a whole and negative growth for the eurozone.[9] OECD data reveal a number of other regional strengths. Even if those numbers only cover six of the eight Nordic-Baltic countries (Latvia and Lithuania not included) they are still interesting to note. GDP per capita is higher than the eurozone, EU and OECD averages.[10] The average unemployment rate for the region is lower than in the euro-

---

[5] Global Peace Index 2011, Vision of Humanity.

[6] Heidelberg Institute for International Conflict Research 2011.

[7] SIPRI Military Expenditure Database, constant (2009) USD.

[8] Transparency International 2011.

[9] IMF World Economic Outlook Database Sept 2011 and European Commission Interim Forecast February 2012. NB8 average projection under 2 percent using EUCOMs figures, over 2 percent using IMF figures.

[10]OECD Factbook 2011, USD, current prices and PPPs, 2009.

zone,[11] and regarding young people who are neither in education nor employment, statistics are also more positive for the Nordic-Baltic region than for the OECD as a whole.[12] Nordic-Baltic productivity is higher than the OECD average.[13] With its relatively small, open economies and export-dependent countries, the Nordic-Baltic region is also a bigger trader than the rest of Europe, with a higher proportion of international trade as part of GDP than both the eurozone and the EU as a whole.[14]

Strategic Strengths

Looking at the situation regarding education, technology and research, the Nordic-Baltic region stands strong compared with other Western countries. Educational expenditure per student is higher in the region than the OECD average[15] and the same applies to the proportion of the population with higher education.[16] The region also scores higher than the OECD average in international student assessments in both math and science.[17] There is greater access for people in the region to both a home computer and the Internet than the OECD average.[18] The proportion of ICT specialists and ICT users among people who work is higher in the Nordic-Baltic region than in most other OECD countries[19] and the proportion of researchers in the work force is significantly higher than for the EU as a whole.[20] In terms of expenditures on research and development, the Nordic-Baltic region scores higher than both the EU as a whole and the OECD average.[21]

---

[11] IMF World Economic Outlook Database September 2011.

[12] OECD Factbook 2011.

[13] Ibid., labor productivity, GDP per hour worked, USD 2010.

[14] Ibid., international trade in goods and services as % of GDP 2010.

[15] Ibid., primary, secondary, post-secondary, tertiary levels 2008.

[16] Ibid., percentage of population aged 25-64 with tertiary education.

[17] Ibid., International Student Assessment, men and women.

[18] Ibid., percentage of households 2009.

[19] Ibid., Luxemburg and the UK rate higher.

[20] Ibid., per 1000 employed 2009.

[21] Eurostat 2012 and OECD Factbook 2011.

A Region with a Bigger Mission?

All these advantages give the Nordic-Baltic region an exceptional starting point as a leading actor in the transatlantic dialogue on common security-related issues. And the more the Nordic-Baltic countries are able to think and act regionally—as opposed to nationally—the bigger their common potential is to play a leading role. The listed strengths of the region also provide the U.S. with a partner (or a grouping of partners) that has a proven track record in pragmatic cooperation, stability, responsibility and strategic investments. With political will, the U.S. and the Nordic-Baltics could break ground on a number of fronts where new dynamics could be useful, for example, regarding Eastern Europe, Russia, energy security, the High North, and transatlantic security strategies in times of financial austerity.

The Nordic-Baltics and the U.S.:
A Relationship of Unique Dynamics

The current U.S.-Nordic-Baltic relationship has evolved with very different starting points for the individual Nordic-Baltic countries. Norway, Denmark, and Iceland joined NATO in 1949 and were close security partners of the United States throughout the Cold War. Sweden and Finland were non-aligned during the Cold War (Sweden nevertheless maintained close relations with the United States). The three Baltic countries, on the other hand, were under Soviet occupation until 1991 when independence was restored, at which point they immediately sought reintegration into the Euro-Atlantic community, entering the EU and NATO in 2004. This process was supported by the Nordic countries and the U.S., *inter alia*, through its 1997 Northern Europe Initiative (NEI).

But the end of the Cold War and the disappearance of the Soviet threat also resulted in the gradual dissipation of the Nordic-Baltic region's strategic importance to Washington. While Denmark, Norway and Iceland continued to prioritize their memberships in NATO, Sweden and Finland retained their policy of non-alignment. However, they both joined NATO's Partnership for Peace program (PfP) in 1994 and the European Union in 1995. Sweden and Finland, as a part of PfP, have collaborated closely with NATO, contributing to its missions and participating in exercises. Moreover, as members of the EU,

Finland and Sweden (together with the other EU members) have been part of the drive towards a more developed security role for the EU. While Denmark had already joined the European Economic Community back in 1973, Norway and Iceland have so far remained outside of the EU (although Iceland is now a candidate).

Despite their different starting points and discrepancies regarding NATO and EU memberships, the countries of the Nordic-Baltic region share a global outlook and engagement. Since October 2003, the U.S. has engaged the Nordic-Baltic region through the Enhanced Partnership in Northern Europe (e-PINE). Replacing the NEI, this policy framework outlines a cooperative, multilateral approach to a host of issues ranging from security to economic growth. And over the past two decades, the Nordic-Baltic countries have made a number of important concrete contributions to global peace and security.

Afghanistan

One important case is Afghanistan. Though the individual contributions may seem modest compared to the U.S. and British forces, taken together the Nordic-Baltic countries in fact make up one of the largest troop contributors to the ISAF force since its establishment at the end of 2001. The combined figure of around 2,500 troops surpasses that of countries such as Australia, Poland, Spain, Turkey, and the Netherlands. Only France, Germany, Italy, UK, and the U.S. sent more troops to ISAF than the Nordic-Baltic countries combined as of October 2011.[22] Furthermore, the Nordic contributions look even more impressive when accounting for population size. The Nordic countries have also made contributions to the EU's EUPOL mission in the country, providing a third of total EU contributions as of July 2011.[23]

Counter-terrorism

In the decade following the September 11 attacks, international cooperation on counter-terrorism emerged as a top U.S. foreign policy priority, influencing Washington's bilateral and multilateral rela-

---

[22]All troop figures are based on the latest ISAF/NATO Placemat, and are current as of 18 October 2011.

[23]http://www.csdpmap.eu/mission-personnel.

tionships. Nordic and Baltic leaders were united in condemning the attacks using the strongest possible language and in expressing solidarity with the United States. Nordic countries were also proactive in endorsing and implementing various counter-terrorism measures introduced in the aftermath of the attacks. In general, bilateral counter-terrorism cooperation between the Nordic-Baltic countries and the United States has been overwhelmingly positive. While friction over some issues such as the Guantanamo Bay detention center and the invasion of Iraq strained the U.S.-Nordic relationship during the Bush years, things appear to have improved notably during the Obama administration. It should also be noted that the Nordic countries have themselves been targets of terrorism during this period.

International Crisis Management

Over the past two decades, the Nordic-Baltic countries have been active in international crisis management. For example, at its peak, the Nordic-Baltic countries contributed a combined 1,858 troops to the KFOR force in Kosovo.[24] During the recent NATO-led air campaign in Libya, the Nordic countries again punched above their weight, with Denmark and Norway each providing six F-16M fighter jets and Sweden eight Jas 29 Gripen planes to the mission.[25] The combined contributions of Denmark, Estonia, Finland, and Sweden to the humanitarian effort in Libya amounted to 25 million euros as of February 2012.[26] As of March 2011, Norway was among the five largest donors to the crisis in Libya.[27]

When it comes to patrolling the coast of Somalia, Denmark and Norway participated in NATO's Operation Ocean Shield while Denmark, Estonia, Lithuania, Finland, and Sweden all participated in the

---

[24] These figures are based on data from the NATO KFOR website. For current numbers see: http://www.nato.int/kfor/structur/nations/placemap/kfor_placemat.pdf.

[25] Sweden only did aerial surveillance whereas Denmark and Norway took part in offensive operations. The Baltic states did not participate in the Libya campaign.

[26] EU DG ECHO, available online at: http://ec.europa.eu/echo/files/aid/countries/libya_factsheet.pdf.

[27] IRIN News "In Brief: Donors pledge $65m for Libyan humanitarian crisis", available online at: http://www.irinnews.org/Report/92121/In-Brief-Donors-pledge-65m-for-Libyan-humanitarian-crisis.

EU NAVFOR Atalanta mission. The region actively supports the EU's Common Security and Defence Policy (CSDP), contributing to its military and civilian missions. Even non-EU member Norway has sent personnel to EU missions and contributed to the Nordic Battle-group, which is considered one of Europe's most prepared crisis response forces. The fact that the NB8 have contributed to both NATO and EU missions also illustrates that the region has come a long way in bridging the organizational divide that is still characterizing European security affairs, something that may thus serve as a model for others to follow.

Besides EU and NATO missions, the Nordic-Baltic countries have been committed to a long tradition of supporting UN "blue helmet" peacekeeping operations. Currently, one or more Nordic-Baltic states is contributing to 9 of the 16 ongoing UN peacekeeping missions.[28] They have also supported many of the OSCE's missions in Europe's neighborhood. In addition, the Nordic nations, particularly Denmark, Finland, and Sweden, have also come a long way in the effort to develop civilian crisis management tools, such as police, judiciary and customs reforms, and capacity building to be used in post-conflict zones.[29]

Humanitarian Assistance and Development

Another area where the Nordic countries are major contributors is humanitarian assistance and development. According to the OECD-DAC, Norway, Finland, Denmark, and Sweden all scored among the world's highest donors per capita. In terms of official development assistance (ODA), the four Nordic countries and Estonia's ODA reached in 2010 15.8 billion USD, roughly equaling the size of the UK, and more than either France or Germany.[30] International disaster response is another area of growing significance where the Nordics have an impressive track record. During the 2010 earthquake in Haiti,

---

[28]Data gathered from website of UN DPKO: http://www.un.org/en/peacekeeping/operations/current.shtml.

[29]For an evaluation of EU civilian crisis management capabilities, see http://www.ecfr.eu/page/-/documents/08e8648caa55523ceb_g2m6yhyrv.pdf.

[30]OCED Development Cooperation Report 2010. Estonia, Latvia, Lithuania are not included in the OECD DAC statistics (although Estonia become a member in 2010).

the four Nordic countries pledged more than France, Germany and the UK combined.[31] During the 2004 Asian tsunami, the Nordic countries were also among the top donors.[32]

Conclusions

The Nordic-Baltic region has a history of pragmatic cooperation and a strong shared commitment to the transatlantic relationship. The countries in the region have significant interests and expertise on issues such as economic and political transitions, cooperation with Russia, energy issues, and the High North. There are good reasons for the countries of the Nordic-Baltic region to consider taking further steps toward strengthening their own regional cooperation and increasingly think in terms of common interests, rather than merely national ones.

Taking into account the range of European strategic security issues still at hand, and the broader need for renewed transatlantic political energy, there are equally good reasons for the U.S. to consider further developing its dialogue and partnership with the Nordic-Baltic region.

With a history of stability and prosperity, shared values and norms and a commitment to pragmatic cooperation, the region is an attractive partner to the U.S. Moreover, the region has a long track record of working together with the U.S. in promoting global peace and security around the world. This often-overlooked insight should provide impetus for an even stronger U.S. engagement with the Nordic-Baltic region.

Naturally, such a strengthened partnership should complement, rather than replace, the broader transatlantic dialogue. With a new perspective on U.S.-Nordic-Baltic cooperation, possibilities may

---

[31]This is based on data from UN OCHA, presented in the Guardian, available online at: http://www.guardian.co.uk/news/datablog/2010/jan/14/haiti-quake-aid-pledges-country-donations.

[32]Congressional Research Report "Indian Ocean Earthquake and Tsunami: Humanitarian Assistance and Relief Operations", January 2005, available online at: http://www.fas.org/sgp/crs/row/RL32715.pdf

emerge to break new ground and lead the way in a number of security-related areas for the benefit of the broader transatlantic community. In this way, the U.S.-Nordic-Baltic format presents an opportunity that should not be missed.

Section I

"A Europe Whole and Free"

Chapter Two

"A Europe Whole and Free"—
A Prophetic Concept
and an Unfinished Business

Adam Daniel Rotfeld

In his memorable speech in Berlin in December 1989, U.S. Secretary of State James Baker said: "Free men and free governments, are the building blocks of a Europe whole and free."[1] The Europe of 2012 corresponds only in part to Baker's vision; Europe is not entirely united and free. International security in the Euro-Atlantic region is defined by common institutions, universal values, and divergent interests. The alliance-based NATO, the community-based EU, and the loose cooperation of the remaining countries within the OSCE and NATO partnerships reflect the reality of the second decade of the 21st century.

Not every country in the Euro-Atlantic region shares the values of political pluralism, free market, the rule of law, media freedom, and respect for human rights. Even if these are accepted in theory, they are rejected in political practice. Cold War rhetoric has returned; the alleged superiority of "non-interference into domestic affairs" over all other principles of the Helsinki Final Act (1975) apparently justifies "sovereign democracy." However if common values—aside from com-

Professor Adam Daniel Rotfeld is former Minister for Foreign Affairs of Poland; member of the Euro-Atlantic Security Commission, Co-Chair of the Polish-Russian Group on Difficult Issues. He conducts academic work at the Institute for Interdisciplinary Studies "Artes Liberales" at the University of Warsaw.

[1] *A New Europe, a New Atlanticism: Architecture for a New Era.* Address by James A. Baker, III, U.S. Secretary of State, to the Berlin Press Club, Berlin, December 12, 1989. Text in: Adam Daniel Rotfeld and Walther Stuetzle (eds): *Germany and Europe in Transition.* SIPRI-Oxford University Press, 1991, p. 96.

mon interests—fail to be respected, the security community will be a mere facade.

The New Strategic Concept of NATO, based on the Report prepared by the Group of Experts led by Madeleine Albright, defined three essential core tasks of the Alliance: collective defense, crisis management, and cooperative security.[2] In other words, the Alliance's new aims and tasks are not only focused on territorial defense of its members but they are oriented to protect the community of values as well, and these are not limited to the Euro-Atlantic area. Its crisis management function is also applicable to other regions of the world.

New security threats are quite often associated with three factors: instability, uncertainty, and unpredictability. They are diverse and complex, and come largely from non-traditional sources (such as violent extremism, terrorism, cyber attacks and proliferation of weapons of mass destruction). What does this mean in a European context?

The Higher the Expectations, the Greater the Disappointment

In their Policy Report of the European Council on Foreign Relations, Ivan Krastev and Mark Leonard made an intellectually provocative and inspiring comment: "The European Union has spent much of the last decade defending a European order that no longer functions while hoping for a global order that will probably never come. As a result, the European continent is less stable than we thought it had become, while the EU is less influential than we hoped it would be."[3] In other words, the higher the expectations, the greater the disappointment. One should not forget, however, that Europe today is more secure than it has ever been. The main problems are not generated so much by the deficit of security, but rather by the lack of trust and mutual confidence, especially in relations between the EU/NATO

---

[2] NATO 2020: Assured Security; Dynamic Engagement. Analysis and Recommendations of the Group of Experts on a New Strategic Concept for NATO. Brussels, 17 May 2010. See Adam Daniel Rotfeld, "NATO 2020: A New Strategic Concept of the Alliance," *The Polish Quarterly of International Affairs*, Vol. 19/4. 2010.

[3] The Spectre of a Multipolar Europe, Policy Report of the European Council. Brussels, October 2010.

members and Russia. The strategic relationship between the EU/NATO and Russia should not be detached from the global political context. If the emerging Euro-Atlantic security order is to be successful, it must adequately respond to the conditions and requirements of its time. In short: institutions must follow the problems—and not the other way around.

The present financial crisis and potential immigration crisis from North Africa revealed the fragility and selfish national (and nationalistic) policies of the European states to a much greater extent than the "classical" military strategic challenges, potential threats, and risks based on our experiences deeply rooted in the past.

Krastev and Leonard are right in saying that Europe is losing its centrality in international politics. As a rule, observers are discussing in this context the new emerging powers (BRIC) and the United States' loss of interest in Europe, and rightly so. However, some other decisive factors are often neglected or simply forgotten.

The first is a kind of European passivism and self-restraint in common foreign and security policy motivated by the lack of a strong political will to become engaged and to assume a responsibility comparable to that taken in the United States.

The second factor reflects the new reality that in the last 20 years most of the fundamental changes in the international security environment were caused by developments within states rather than between them.

And the third is a need to be more proactive than reactive—since the main category defining security in our time is not so much stability (as happened in the bipolar system), but transformation, transition, and change. Consequently, the main question is: how should this change be managed?

American Military Presence and Engagement in Europe

At the 48th Munich Security Conference (February 4, 2012) U.S. Secretary of Defense Leon E. Panetta discussed the key elements of the new American defense strategy, stating:

First, the United States military will be smaller and we will be leaner. (...) But what we wanted to stress was a force that would be agile, that would be flexible, that would be rapidly deployable, and that would be technologically advanced. It must be a cutting edge force for the future.

Second, we will enhance our presence in Asia Pacific and the Middle East, where we see the greatest challenges and the greatest opportunities in the 21st century.

Third, we will maintain a robust presence in Europe and elsewhere in the world by investing in existing alliances, by helping to make them stronger, by developing new partnerships, and by developing new innovative rotational deployments that will give us the capability to have a presence not only in Europe, but in Africa and Latin America and elsewhere.

Fourth, we will ensure that we can quickly confront and defeat aggression from any adversary, any time, any place. It is essential that we have the capability to deal with more than one adversary at a time (...).

And fifth, we will protect and prioritize key investments— key investments in technology and new capabilities from special operations forces to cyber and space and unmanned systems, as well as our capacity to surge, adapt and grow as needed.[4]

For Europe, the U.S. Secretary of Defense confirmed strongly that the American footprint "will remain larger than in any other region in the world. (...) Europe remains our security partner, our security partner of choice for military operations and diplomacy around the world."[5]

In short, the two new elements of the U.S. security strategy as defined by Defense Secretary Panetta are: American military presence and engagement in Europe—it will be leaner militarily and reoriented from the Atlantic to the Pacific. This is for one simple reason: there is no direct military threat in Europe, but there is in Asia and in some other regions of the world.

---

[4] http://www.defense.gov/transcripts/transcript.aspx?transcriptid=4972

[5] Ibid.

Emergence of New Security Systems

New security systems do not emerge from "round-table" discussions, even if these attract the most prominent attendees as was the case in Munich. Their visions, concepts and proposals may indeed be drawn upon by politicians in helping to systematize and harmonize various, and often contradictory, state interests. But their decisive purpose is to properly identify and reconcile three fundamental elements, which are characteristic of any security system. These are: interests, values, and power.

In the past, new systems were usually agreed upon fairly quickly—after the end of large-scale wars. The victors enforced and imposed their will upon the defeated. That is how—after the Napoleonic wars—the Holy Alliance and the Concert of Powers came into being in Europe; their concept designed by the Austrian Chancellor Metternich. And although his goal was mainly to achieve hegemony for Austria, many politicians still regard the system then created as a model for international power relations. After all, it produced stability and peace for several generations. Similar ambitions were harbored by the signatories of the 1856 Paris Peace Treaty, who met 22 years later in Berlin to revise the provisions of the San Stefano Peace Treaty between Russia and Turkey.

The winners of the First World War, in turn, dictated the terms of the Versailles Treaty (1919), laying the foundation for a new security system. An attempt was then made for the multilateral institutionalization of the system in the form of the League of Nations. But, for many reasons, that organization failed to live up to expectations, and did not prevent Hitler's *Neue Ordnung* from being imposed on Europe. As illustrated by appeasement and the Munich Treaty, this policy went unopposed by the Western democracies. Concessions to the aggressor culminated in the division and conquest of Europe, beginning with the Molotov-Ribbentrop Pact and the outbreak of the Second World War. The end of that war gave rise to yet another system based on the treaties of Yalta and Potsdam and, later on, the United Nations Charter.

The Paris Charter for a New Europe (November 1990), more so than any other document, identified the important new feature of an emerging international system, a feature which boils down to this simple observation: in the 21st century, international security in the global and regional dimension—especially European—is contingent more on the situation within states rather than between them.

The nature of conflicts has changed, and this is a development from which conclusions should now be drawn. Discussions about the new system must not ignore the observation that over the past twenty years nearly all armed conflicts have broken out within states, not between them. From a strictly military point of view, these are usually low-intensity conflicts. Increasingly, they are of an asymmetrical nature, where parties include not only states but also non-state actors.

Confidence and conviction in the possibility that the international system can be shaped in a model way is widespread, and ensues from the need to impose order on a complex subject matter perceived as a world of chaos, uncertainty and instability. In effect, after the breakdown of the bipolar system, two diametrically opposed concepts emerged: the model of unipolarity, which in essence constituted an attempt to describe the new role of the United States as the dominant and hegemonic power in the contemporary world; and the model of multipolarity, which implicitly presupposed the division of the world into spheres of influence among global powers. In other words, instead of two centers of gravity (Washington and Moscow) the new model presupposed either a unipolar system with a hegemonic position for the United States, or a multipolar system with specific privileges for the great powers, which have pretences of imposing their will upon states within their sphere of interests and influence. This constituted a search for a new kind of directorate—a new Concert of Powers that would rule the world. Such searching is based on the premise that polarity is, in essence, an eternal or immemorial idea which puts into order the international community. In reality, the bipolar world was an exception to the rule. It was merely a reflection of a specific historical situation that took shape following the Second World War, when the two largest victorious powers (the United States and the Soviet Union) not only relied on enormous nuclear arsenals sufficient to assure mutual destruction, but also formed the center of gravity for two opposing social and political systems. The concept of mutual deterrence, whose premise had been the high probability that a nuclear conflict would break out, was also accompanied by a high degree of stabilization. The "armed peace" presupposed the maintenance of the territorial and political status quo in the regions dominated by the two political and military blocs.

The new international political and military environment differs fundamentally from the situation that was the cause and source of the Cold War between East and West. The new reality is incomparably more complex, and any attempts to steer or 'manage' the world in keeping with a political philosophy of rival power centers are tantamount to accepting a kind of polycentric concept of security. In military terms, the United States and Russia (as the successor state to the Soviet Union) have long since lost their nuclear monopoly. Furthermore the nuclear non-proliferation regime seriously eroded, and nuclear weapons are now in the hands not only of the five great powers—the members of the UN Security Council—but also in those of India, Pakistan and Israel.

Robert Cooper was right when he wrote that, "This is a new world, but there is neither a new world order (...) nor is there a new disorder."[6] There is a safe Europe and a safe North America, but there are areas from which threats emanate, not only for individual regions (the Persian Gulf, the Middle East, the Korean Peninsula), but for the world as a whole. There are also areas of chaos, a lack of prospects for development, uncertainty, poverty, famine and disease (Africa, and many countries of Asia and Latin America).

In the opinion of Henry Kissinger (a classic practitioner of *Realpolitik*), there are two paths to stability: hegemony or equilibrium. Such thinking about challenges reflects older times. In the diversified yet interdependent world of the 21st century, it is futile to refer to the simple schemes and logical thought patterns that corresponded to the needs of the 19th century and to the first half of the 20th. Their application, while failing to address present problems, creates new ones instead.

---

[6] Robert Cooper, *The Breaking of Nations. Order and Chaos in the Twenty-First Century*, Atlantic Monthly Press, London 2003, p. 55.

Unconventional Problems and Situations
Call for Unconventional Solutions

In practice, this means that we need to realize that just as the world is diversified, the methods for neutralizing risks and threats are similarly complex. International security necessitates a holistic approach, not only encompassing the political and military dimension (as was the case in the past), but also taking into account economics, information technology, and civilization issues, and allowing nations to protect and cultivate their identities. For the countries of the European Union, the key criterion is respect for the rule of law. For the world as a whole, the organizing idea for global security is interdependence. The fundamental challenges, defined 40 years ago by Karl Deutsch[7], remain significant: mutual relations between nations and states on the one hand, and between societies and the international community on the other.

In this context a legitimate question is raised: what kind of place is there for Russia in her strategic partnership with NATO and the European Union? The response cannot be constructed with only objective factors in mind: Russia's size (the biggest territory in the world) and huge natural resources (especially gas and oil) must both be considered. A crucial element of political analysis is the most subjective and relevant factor, namely Russia's self-perception as a global power legitimized to construct the new transatlantic security architecture based on three pillars (U.S., EU and Russia). Whether a strategy to induce Russia to shift its outlook and foreign policy behavior closer to what the EU considers cooperative and based on a common set of values is to be effective is an open question. A response cannot be made by one party—it has to be a joint and common EU-Russia project.

More than 60 countries in the world, including Russia, France, and the United States, will host elections in 2012. We are living in a time when politicians often know how to fix difficult problems, but later have trouble winning at the polls. Genuine leaders—Churchill, de Gaulle, de Gasperi, Brandt—took decisions in line with long-term

---

[7] Karl Deutsch, *The Analysis of International Relations*, Chapter 1—'Ten Fundamental Questions', Prentice Hall, Englewood Cliffs, New Jersey 1968.

national and global interests. They made the right decisions—but often lost power as a result.

Many politicians consider power a value in itself. They often resort to populist rhetoric and nationalism. As a result we are confronted with a real threat of a kind of "re-nationalization" of foreign and security policies not only outside but also inside the Euro-Atlantic region.

In his recently published book, Zbigniew Brzezinski writes that Russians share Western values, but these are not expressed in its political system.[8] The street protests in Russian cities reflect the contradictions which exist between the young generation's awareness and a political system which hampers development. Russia is not an exception. Uncertainty and loss of trust of the governed means that a number of European countries are feeling increasingly nostalgic about the idea of renationalizing security; namely, returning to the national niche. The generation which now has both say and power sees the experiences of World War Two and postwar development as little but a piece of distant history.

Russia and Turkey should be integrated into the Euro-Atlantic security community. The Russian elite would like to see closer ties with the European Union and NATO, but is not willing to implement the kind of domestic reforms that would make these ties possible. Professor Brzezinski claims, however, that a rapprochement will take place within the next 20 years.

Indeed, Russia needs the West; the West needs Russia—but only a Russia whose system is based on common values: the rule of law and respect for democratic governance.

The Path Toward Cooperative Security

On February 4, 2012, at the Munich Security Conference, a similar political philosophy was presented by the authors of a report published by the Euro-Atlantic Security Initiative (EASI). This is a blueprint for a system based on trust and cooperation which may make

---

[8] Zbigniew Brzezinski: *Strategic Vision: America and the Crisis of Global Power*. Basic Books. New York 2012.

Russia an ally of the West.[9] Even though 20 years have elapsed since the end of the Cold War, its authors claim that Europe is neither fully united nor fully free.

The bonds between the United States and Europe are weakening. U.S. decisions to reduce its military presence in Europe, the reduction in military spending, and the deployment of more troops in the Pacific region mean that European security must be guaranteed under these new conditions. The sovereign debt crisis and radical military spending cuts in France and Britain are not making matters any easier.

Yet the authors of the EASI report believe that since the Western world managed to guarantee European security in the aftermath of World War Two—at a time of deep-running ideological divisions, military conflicts, and the looming threat of a nuclear war—it will be all the more possible today, now that those divisions have disappeared and the possibility of nuclear confrontation is close to zero. Indeed, if Franco-German and Polish-German reconciliation has been a success, then sooner or later we will achieve an understanding with Russia.

Although old threats (e.g. proliferation of WMDs) have not quite disappeared and new ones have emerged (terrorism, energy shortages, cyber insecurity), the main obstacle on the path toward cooperative security is the crisis of trust and leadership. "What was a good idea two years ago has now become a political imperative," wrote the report's authors.

First of all, we must realize that Russian and Western security is increasingly less dependent on the military factor, and that the future is about mutual trust. This constitutes a difficult task, especially when we consider that over the next decade Russia is planning to boost its military spending by USD 600 billion, while the United States has announced defense budget cuts to the tune of more than USD 500 billion.

Furthermore, conflicted parties must sit down at one table: these include Russia and its neighbors, Turkey and Armenia, Moldova and Transnistria, or the Greek and Turkish Cypriot communities.

---

[9] Toward a Euro-Atlantic Security Community. EASI Final Report published by the Carnegie Endownment for International Peace. Washington DC, February 2012.

In order to break the deadlock in these cases, the authors of the EASI report suggest implementing initiatives in the area of military, human and energy security.

Trust in the military domain would be founded on increasing early warning and decision-making times, explaining operational doctrines, and sharing information about partners' military capabilities and resources. In a nutshell: based on understanding each other's intentions.

The principal "apple of discord" between the West and Russia is missile defense. Russia's stance is motivated by the balance of power concept and geopolitics. In November 2011, President Dmitry Medvedev announced the deployment of new missiles in the Kaliningrad Oblast.

The joint project to break this impasse has been put forward by an EASI-based group of politicians and generals.[10] The architectural design was jointly created by a former director of the U.S. Department of Defense's Missile Defense Agency and former chief of staff of the USSR Strategic Rocket Forces. Their report claims that breaking the impasse in negotiations and the "transformation of the very essence of relations" between the U.S. and Russia in this sphere must be given priority status by the two governments. The authors provide principles for Russian-Western cooperation on missile defense. They call for the drafting of a joint program to prevent the most serious threats, currently posed by medium-range ballistic missiles (max. range 4,500 km). Such cooperation would ensure a more effective response to threats than a strategy implemented independently by one country. Joint action means that NATO and Russia would create joint data and information exchange centers, and that both sides would protect their territory while enabling the interception of passing missiles aimed at a partner country.[11]

---

[10]The new cooperative NATO-Russia approach was elaborated by Steve Hadley, former U.S. President National Security Advisor; Volker Rühe, former Defence Minister of Germany; Vyacheslav Trubnikov, former Director of the Russian Foreign Intelligence Service.

[11]Attached to the EASI report are five detailed analyses. Two of these describe political solutions to "frozen" conflicts and reconciliation between adversaries, as well as a new approach to arms control covering both strategic and tactical nuclear weapons. The two remaining analyses concern energy security and the place and role of Turkey in

The reports' conclusions consist of specific postulates, calling on the U.S., EU and Russian authorities to accept—even before the NATO Summit in Chicago in May 2012—the vision of a Euro-Atlantic security community as the foundation of their political philosophy, and to instruct their senior military commanders and defense officials to create "a dynamic confidence-building process to lengthen warning and decision-making time in both of Europe's military spheres—conventional and nuclear."

They advocate the resumption of military exchanges and joint missile defense exercises held under the auspices of the NATO-Russia Council. They also suggest taking Nelson Mandela's example and creating a Group of Elders, which would reinvigorate the OSCE process of resolving "protracted" conflicts between Chisinau and Tiraspol in Moldova, and between Armenia and Azerbaijan in Nagorno-Karabakh.

The report's authors also claim that in order to achieve reconciliation between Russia and its neighbors—especially Poland and the Baltic States—it is imperative that archives be opened. They also recommend that Russia and the EU establish a joint energy innovation and efficiency centre, and enhance the mechanism created in 2009, which issues early warnings in the event of disruptions of gas supplies. The list also includes the gradual abolition of the visa requirement and the coordination of Arctic security policy.

The world is changing faster than our ability to comprehend the essence of these changes. The United States, China and Russia are all searching for their new place in the world. The "pivot" of global politics is shifting from Europe and the Atlantic to Asia and the Pacific.

Europe's global role will depend on the Europeans themselves. For now they seem preoccupied with themselves. The fiscal crisis is taking precedence over matters of military security.

---

the proposed Euro-Atlantic community. Some new recommendations are elaborated by the Working Groups on Historical Reconciliation and Protracted Conflicts, Energy as a Building Block in Creating a Euro-Atlantic Security Community; and two papers addressing Nonstrategic Nuclear Forces and The Turkish Dimension in Creating a Euro-Atlantic Security Community.

Core Challenges to Security

A Euro-Atlantic Security Initiative Commission co-chaired by Nunn, Ivanov, and Ischinger offers an innovative approach to the question of how to establish an inclusive, undivided security space free of opposing blocks and grey areas. In their view, five core challenges, as presented by them in the interim report, must be confronted head-on.

First, U.S.-Russian and NATO-Russian security relations must, as a conscious goal, be converted from residual hostility and strategic rivalry to strategic cooperation. This can only be done by introducing greater communication, mutual understanding and restraint in their military relations.

Second, a historic reconciliation within the Euro-Atlantic area's eastern half comparable to that achieved by its western half must be consciously pursued. As part of this process, the security of Ukraine, Georgia, Moldova, and other new states must be assured and the area's frozen conflicts resolved.

Third, the dueling narratives agitating relations among Euro-Atlantic countries must give way to a new narrative recognizing the substantial stakes in the growing security and prosperity of all, and the considerable risk in the weakness and tribulations of any member.

Fourth, a path to Euro-Atlantic energy security based on interdependence rather than competition must be pursued.

Finally, the institutions on which the Euro-Atlantic states rely for security must be modified, strengthened and welded into a division of labor enabling them all to meet the 21st century's new security challenges.

The creation of a genuine security community is feasible.

The world as we know it is becoming a thing of the past. The outlines of a new global order—which lives up to the challenges ahead—are becoming ever sharper. These challenges include fundamental changes in the role played by individuals and societies in the new cyberspace. The market for political ideas is seeing a rise in demand for imagination and reason. Three factors, however, should be seen as the points of departure in a search for achieving the aims of the 1989 project "A Europe Whole and Free": NATO should remain the key organization responsible for the collective defense and security of the Euro-Atlantic community; the effectiveness of the European foreign and security policy depends on unity and alliance between big and small European countries; and—last but not least—the transatlantic Alliance and the European Union are together the only multilateral institutions that can facilitate, in a common and optimum way, peaceful development and prosperity for Europe, North America and Russia while guaranteeing their security in an uncertain and unstable world.

Chapter Three
I'll Gladly Pay You Tuesday

Toomas Hendrik Ilves

Slowly, ever so slowly, we are realizing, or at least should be, that the fundamental reordering of Europe that began with the crumbling collapse of an overextended and unsustainable communist glacis in the late 1980s has had far greater and far-reaching reverberations than we then would or could have predicted.

Soviet-style communism, even in the short run an unworkable form of despotism since its imposition in 1917, remained so through its iteration by military force and occupation in Eastern Europe in the 1940s. We know that crony capitalism leads to economic busts, but crony communism never really even gets off the ground; just seedy privilege—bigger bad cars, better bad health care, better bad education for the children of the well-connected—justified not by achievement but by self-appointment to bring about a more radiant future, because only the self-appointed party is capable of giving hope of a better future. We will shortly meet this phrase again.

Deng Xiaoping realized already in the late 1970s, a decade before the collapse of what by then was simply a Soviet *khrushchyovka* of worn-out cards that a society or a country cannot borrow on the future, that productive creative labor is what must be allowed, and that privilege without merit leads to Soviet-style stagnation. Deng realized social stratification based on party membership, not on accomplishment, was unsustainable and proclaimed: "It is glorious to get rich." He didn't say, nota bene, that it is glorious to have free speech and free and fair elections. China realized it needed to change and embraced

Toomas Hendrik Ilves is the president of Estonia. He has previously served as Estonian foreign minister, member of the European Parliament, and the ambassador of Estonia in Washington. This is an abridged version of a longer essay published in the April/May 2012 issue of *Policy Review*, published by the Hoover Institution.

capitalism without democracy. Moscow was more obtuse, at least until the second half of the 1980s.

In the West even fewer got it, telling themselves that East Europeans really liked to be enserfed, and for most of my adult life, I found that people in the West actually had come to believe it. Happy Estonians building the Baikal Amur highway, wholesome Polish plumbers, tanned Lithuanian *kolkhozniks* bringing in the sheaves somehow lulled people into believing it was "an alternative," a different way to do things toward which we too would move in some kind of utopian convergence. But then communism collapsed and Western Europe was faced with its "Uh-oh, now what?" problem: all those poor cousins at its doorstep and no more barbed wire, wall, or indeed any other kind of gate. A continent of exiles—people who talked about communism just the way the excoriated "emigrés" from the East had been talking, unpleasantly, uncomfortably for all those years. And even those who didn't buy the convergence myth or the silly Campaign for Nuclear Disarmament line—about Russians loving their children, too, and therefore Moscow harbored no ill will toward the West, and maybe for them freedom of speech is just another term for nothing left to say—well, they were stung.

For 50 years since the Atlantic Charter, those of us East and West who didn't believe it was all okay instead believed the rhetoric that we would all be one were it not for the evil Soviet Union and its lack of democracy, and that we could redeem ourselves from the graceless half century by working hard, speaking freely, following the rules, and doing our homework. We believed that Western Europe yearned for us as we yearned for it, as Aristophanes described in Plato's *Symposium*, two halves of a whole split by the gods, perpetually seeking our other half, to live in a Europe whole and free.

It turned out to be much more complicated. With the end of communism it was time to redeem those bonds and vouchers of the ideologized 1940s, 50s, 60s, 70s and 80s. We discovered that to Western Europe the liberation of enserfed and silenced Easterners turned out instead to mean "social dumping" by Polish plumbers in France, and "lazy Latvian" construction workers in Sweden, and in our case—to believe some Finnish newspapers from as late as Spring 2011, "criminals from Tallinn" disembarking each night in Helsinki harbor by the hundreds—or, the expression I heard in Munich already in 1990 from my *Hausmeisterin* after my bicycle was stolen, *Heute gestohlen, morgen in Polen* (stolen today, tomorrow in Poland).

Liberation and what ensued turned out to be a conundrum expressed in the German Wessie's pride: "Look at all I have accomplished through hard work" and the Ossie's bitter response: "You were lucky to have that opportunity." Except now we in the East who took the exhortations to frugality, discipline, hard work, and following the rules have discovered that while the West German truly worked hard, saved, and made his country a success, others merely borrowed and inflated their gdp through borrowing.

The view of Eastern "wogs" being the culprits in Europe's difficulties is an attitude with amazing persistence. Its history stretches back centuries; it was resurrected with particular vehemence in the past twenty years, and while we thought it would fade with EU enlargement, it turns out to be as robust as ever. Just this past November, Jean-Claude Piris, formerly legal counsel of the European Council and a man frequently described as an architect of the EU, claimed in the *Financial Times* that at fault for all of the EU's financial woes is the too rapid enlargement of Europe to include the formerly communist part. Therefore, he said, we need a two-speed Europe, "because the EU cannot afford to be cast as a symbol of austerity. It must offer a broader political project, capable of giving hope of a *better* future" (my italics).

In translation, if you didn't get it: What we Easterners call not living beyond our means is not as important as putting on "offer a broader political project, capable of giving hope of a better future." Don't create real value, borrow instead; cook the books, lie to Eurostat, live off others' frugality. It is justified in the name of a "better future." This is the kind of talk we heard in Eastern Europe for fifty years. To justify oppressing their subjugated subjects and their own privileged lives, communists spoke constantly of the Radiant Future as a political project . . . capable of giving hope of a better future. This radiant future, this hope, alas, was always receding. It wasn't the communists' fault, though, that it didn't arrive; it was the fault of communism's "five enemies": the four seasons, and international imperialism. Or saboteurs. Or bourgeois remnants. Following the same (il)logic, it is today we, the East Europeans, who are to blame for the borrowing policies of some older member states.

As a child I would watch on my refugee parents' second-hand black-and-white tv reruns of Popeye, a World War II-era American cartoon whose primary message seemed to be that eating spinach made you strong. One supporting character, Wimpy, was a pot-bellied sad-sack whose only line, repeated from cartoon to cartoon, sums up the attitude that led us in Europe to where we are today: "I'll gladly pay you Tuesday for a hamburger today."

Of course, we need not impute to all of the EU what an "an architect of the EU" says, but we know from the housing projects and council estates that ring the city of every formerly communist country what bad architecture can produce. More importantly, we know how widespread this attitude in fact and unfortunately is.

The question that arises is: Who will pay for Wimpy's hamburger today? For that matter, how will Wimpy pay Tuesday? The problem Europe now faces is whether it can maintain this ever-receding dream of a radiant future and paying on Tuesday. I am particularly concerned by the chorus of whispers that financial responsibility is a threat to democracy, that the democracies in some countries that have to undergo severe fiscal adjustment cannot withstand these calls for financial probity. That, as the architect implies, democracy in Europe is something that others must pay for, an attitude repeated in obscene caricatures of Angela Merkel bedecked in a swastika.

It strikes me as especially odd that anyone should be speaking of too rapid enlargement. We Easterners will not be, if the Commission's current plans for the eu's next Multiannual Financial Framework remain, even equal before 2028, a quarter century after enlargement in 2004. Today countries like mine or Poland have been in the EU for as long as Sweden, Finland, and Austria were when we joined. Yet no one referred to them then as "new" members. The persistence of the East-West divide within the EU to this day smacks of a politically correct dogma students have picked up in, say, their schools of architecture.

The foregoing discussion is Eurocentric. Perhaps too much so. It does not take into account everything else that is changing no less rapidly than the collapse of confidence in the ability of profligate European states to pay back the money with which they financed their borrowed prosperity.

Much else has changed in the twenty-plus years since the collapse of communism in Eastern Europe. Today, the fact that China is becoming the largest economy in the world is already in sight. Already that small percentage of Chinese enjoying a Western standard of living—let us be conservative and say 10 percent—is a population the size of Germany and France combined. Brazil, India, and Turkey should also be generating growth-envy in Europe.

The rise of China, however, has had one profound impact too often ignored in discussions that focus narrowly on the economic importance of that country: on Europe's relations with the United States, the principal political and security partner of Europe since World War II. For much of these past 70 years (or at least after the end of the Marshall Plan), the U.S. has been Europe's foil, the contrasting "other," a counterpoint with which to distinguish oneself, set oneself apart from the crudities of Popeye. Jacques Derrida and Jürgen Habermas in 2003 even proposed that anti-Americanism be the foundation of the beginning of a genuine European foreign policy (patronizingly chastising East Europeans for being so churlish as to support the United States).

Be careful what you ask for. For indeed we are getting it, the U.S. is receding from Europe, reorienting itself to the Pacific. "Re-prioritizing" would be a more neutral term, but it is a withdrawal, a disengagement, a reorientation, an abandonment of romance and idealism and a turn to realism, hard-headed and rational.

We Europeans all misjudged. European anti-Americanism for half a century among the cultural and often political elite was sustained by the implicit assumption of a permanent and hence easy-to-belittle presence. They can be bashed because they would always be over here. Pro-Americanism, Eastern or Western, was simplistic, un-European, a sign that you were not quite right or a stooge. Politicians forgot that national interest and contributions in troops, materiel, and finances, not assumed commonality of values, are what sustain an alliance.

We here in Europe and even our friends, the transatlanticists in Washington, now realize that the U.S. presence, its interest in us, was not a done deal forever. Indeed, now that it is drawing—has drawn?—to a close, it is worthwhile to recall that for a long time, we were the most important partner for America. Henry Luce in 1941 famously declared the 20th century the "American Century," calling upon the U.S. to abandon its isolationism and to defend democracy beyond its borders. So it did. And the next 70 years in American foreign policy represented an uncharacteristically "European Century" for Americans.

This, we must realize and face up to, is changing. Completely. More than twenty years after the fall of communism in Eastern Europe, the generation of political leaders with firsthand Cold War and European experience has passed from the scene. Even for those for whom détente or rollback represent more than textbook terms, the period from 1989 to 2004 was a mopping up operation to get countries firmly into the democratic fold after 50 years of totalitarianism: NATO expanded, the EU enlarged.

From the American perspective, "mission accomplished" captured the sentiment. Europe had ceased to be a problem, or at least one the best and brightest in Washington lost sleep over. With China rising to claim its place as a superpower, replacing the ever-less meddling, more middling Russia; with al-Qaeda, the threat of proliferation of WMD and terrorists attacking the U.S. proper, it was assumed that Europe would do its share. At least in its own backyard.

Today the U.S. has other problems, real problems, and if they have one in Europe it's that we don't want to pay our part of our own defense or contribute the necessary manpower or equipment. Decreasing European military capacity, combined with the absence of any threat emanating from Europe, and serious threats indeed coming from the Middle East, Central Asia, and China, means that we in Europe are not high on the agenda. The transatlantic relationship has no passion, and as this trend continues, we Europeans will find we no longer have a real constituency in this or the next administration, Congress, the media, or public opinion.

Of course we can always find a problem, if we try hard enough, that will get Washington's attention. We seem to be doing just that right now with our handling of Europe's financial crisis. The U.S. has woken up to how dependent its financial and economic health is on what happens today in Greece and Italy. Yet it is hardly comforting for

Europeans that the choice seems to be between an America disengaged from Europe and an America reengaged because Europe is in crisis.

We are in the midst of an ongoing and fundamental reordering of Europe. Which means that we can and indeed must do those things that we have feared to do in the past.

A primary issue here is the fundamental divergence in the EU between institutional arrangements and performance. There is increasing talk of a "two-speed Europe," a division between the EU-17 (the countries that use the euro, with the attendant treaty obligations) and a slower noneuro periphery. Yet it strikes me that the institutionalized, treaty-based "Euro-group" is within its confines far more heterogeneous than the EU-27; that within the EU-27 there is an altogether different and separate subset, a coalescence (if not yet a coalition) based on fiscal responsibility: low deficits, low borrowing, a willingness to make needed changes in policy to ensure competitiveness and sustainable growth.

I cannot be the only one to be struck by the glaring fact that the Nordic-Baltic-6, comprising two Eurozone countries, Finland and Estonia, and four non-Eurozone countries, Latvia, Lithuania, Sweden, and Denmark, actually share much more in attitudes and choices than the Eurozone overall. All six countries are for sound spending and borrowing policies, all six have shown a willingness to undertake needed reforms. We who are in the Eurozone in the NB-6 have a fundamental obligation to ensure that the common interests of our neighbors are not ignored by the EU-17. Of course we in Estonia also anxiously await the EU-17 to become an EU-19 and an EU-21 with Latvia and Lithuania, as well as Sweden and Denmark, taking their place at the Eurozone table, which today is becoming an ever more important decision-making body within the EU. Moreover, Poland, outside of the eurogroup, follows fiscal policies more in line with the NB-6 and its eurogroup members than a number of euro-using countries.

Of course, our geographies and geometries are far more complex. Within the euro or EU-17 there is a divide between (on one side) Germany, Austria, Finland, and the Netherlands, a core of Triple-a, net-payers, plus a second tier of Slovenia, Slovakia, and Estonia, neither Triple-a nor net-payer (yet) but nonetheless sticklers for fiscal discipline and following the rules. And on the other side, countries such as Greece, Italy, Spain, and Portugal that for a variety of reasons have failed to follow the rules. In between there are euro-area members such as aaa Luxembourg, aa+ France, and aa Belgium, net-payers (at least as of the next financial period) whose positions on fiscal discipline are somewhat more ambiguous. Finland's European Minister, Alexander Stubb, has proposed a new "geometry" according to which political leadership in the Union would rest with the triple-A group.

All of these versions of "variable geometries" represent possible futures, not clear choices. The probability of the various outcomes will change dramatically with the fortunes of the euro and the ability and willingness of countries to enact necessary reforms that, as Estonians know from our own experience, are necessarily unpopular, at least in the short run.

We would not be in the mess we are in today in Europe if a large number of fellow member states had not taken a fundamentally different tack to thrift, deficits, and borrowing than what they themselves agreed to only a couple of years earlier. My country would never, ever have been able to adopt the euro had we done what was standard operating procedure among many members of the EU-17. At the same time, I would aver that there is little in the fundamental approach taken by Germany, the Netherlands, Estonia, Finland, or Austria that differs from what such noneuro countries as Sweden, Denmark, and Poland have been doing.

Thus the institutional arrangements and the behavior of countries do not jibe. I submit this is unsustainable. Ultimately, the inability or unwillingness of parts of the EU-17 to submit to agreed-upon rules will be defended by an appeal to the position that "our democracy cannot withstand the kind of austerity demanded of us." The first shoots of this position we have already seen emerge. Yet let us be clear about what this means: Fiscally responsible countries will be asked to support fiscally profligate countries in the name of democracy.

You can do it for a while, but if you are a country like Estonia, where the GDP per capita is almost the same as Greece but where the average salary is lower than the Greek minimum wage, and where the pensions and agricultural supports within an internal market are three times lower, it is a matter of time before our voters revolt. The government in my country and the opposition voted to support the European Financial Stability Facility to aid a country richer than us and profligate. Three quarters of the parliament voted in favor. But, note: 75 percent of the population was against.

Here we see in my own country the first seeds of the populism that has recently caused concern throughout the north—in the Netherlands, in Denmark, in Sweden, and most recently also in Finland. Sorry, it's not just the democracies of the south that are under threat. The bankrolling of Southern Europe has already and ever-increasingly threatened the fiscally responsible countries, the ones who have shown solidarity and voted to commit to bailing out those better off than we. Moreover, while much has been made of the change of governments in countries that broke the rules, far too little attention has been paid to what to my mind is a far more significant reverberation: the fall of a responsible, poor, new member state government coalition (in Slovakia) that made the hard choice and voted to support a country richer than it is, all for the sake of European solidarity.

That I submit is a problem, a serious problem and a threat to Europe we have only begun to realize. When we still talk about new and old members, we still talk nonsense about "populism" in all the wrong ways. Indeed I believe that the "populism" and the "specter of the 30s" that all kinds of pundits unknowledgeably appeal to has nothing to do with the populism we see in Northern Europe. That is not a populism of the dispossessed, the unemployed. It is a populism more akin to what Calvin and Luther appealed to than what the fascists of the 1930s appealed to. It is, like most populism, based on resentment, and resentment at unfairness. But the unfairness is, as it was in the 16th Century, a resentment of those who flaunt their flouting the rules by which others abide. Resentment on the part of those who take commitments seriously regarding those who do not: Is that the "specter of the 30s?"

I cannot and will not accept any labels applied to Northern Europeans for being "populists" when they have been doing exactly what has been asked of them. The price of following the rules for a "poor" country like Estonia has been harsh. Yet if we subtract the fake wealth of the "rich," the ones who today cannot pay their debts, who have borrowed their wealth, are they that much richer than we? If part of being European is playing by the rules, that is, following the rule of law, then how can "European Solidarity" ever take precedence over the rules? It is a tough one.

Estonia, I firmly believe, should not only do its part, it should be one of the more understanding countries regarding others with difficulties. Solidarity, after all, was what we were denied in 1940, and our belief in the need for European solidarity is what lies at the core of the Estonian belief in Europe. But for it to work—in Estonia, in Poland, in the other "new countries" who have been EU members long enough to be taken seriously—we need an end to categories that bear no relation to reality. Indeed, we should be among those in the forefront explaining that unless Europe understands responsibility there will be no solidarity, that there is no possibility any longer to promise to pay anyone Tuesday for a hamburger today.

Chapter Four

Nordic-Baltic-U.S.:
Building on Success, Looking Towards the East

Edward Lucas

Security and freedom are the mainstays of cooperation among the U.S.-Nordic-Baltic nine (USNB9). Security means dealing with Europe's only remaining hard security problem: Russia's military capability against the Baltic states. It also means maintaining the integrity of the region's economic, political, judicial, and social fabric against corruption and manipulation from the East. Freedom is shorthand for promoting Euro-Atlantic values of political freedom and the rule of law in Russia, Belarus, Ukraine, Moldova, and elsewhere in the former Soviet Union.

In both these tasks the USNB9 are an untidy mix but a good fit. The world's military superpower stands shoulder to shoulder with military minnows such as Iceland. Two countries in the USNB9 are not in NATO; two are not in the EU. One of the EU members (Denmark) has an opt-out from the EU's common security and foreign policy. Only two countries (Finland and Estonia) are in the euro. The USNB9 include founder members of NATO and "new" ones; countries that joined the EU as early as 1973 (Denmark) and as late as 2004. The legal systems vary, as do living standards and taxation levels. Three big countries with a claim to be "Baltic"—Germany, Poland and Russia—take no part in USNB cooperation.

The diversity is useful. It means that the USNB9 have fingers in lots of pies; at least one of its members belongs to just about every important club in the world, from the Arctic Council to the Antarctic Treaty Consultative Meeting. It is also deceptive, because what unites

---

Edward Lucas is International Editor of the *Economist* and author of "Deception," a new book about east-west espionage

the countries—common values and outlook—is more important than the categories that divide them.

The USNB countries are outward looking and economically vigorous. The European members belong to what might be called "solvent Europe"—the minority of European countries where government bond auctions are of interest only to financiers, not politicians. (Other members of that rather small club are principally Austria, Czech Republic, Germany, the Netherlands, Poland, Slovakia, Slovenia, and Switzerland). Latvia and Lithuania are the economically weakest by far—but even they have won plaudits for their determination in dealing with the fallout from the economic crisis. President Barack Obama was so impressed with Latvia's record that he telephoned Prime Minister Valdis Dombrovskis to congratulate him on his election victory in 2010.

They are also countries where citizens demand good government. They revere free speech and equality before the law. Public tolerance of corruption is low; bribery is not part of daily life. Bureaucrats are expected to be honest; those that enrich themselves or do favors for their families are subject to legal sanction and social censure. Problems do exist; say in city government in places such as New Orleans or Tallinn. But that is quite different from the clientelist culture of, say Greece or Italy. In short, the USNB9 are countries where the citizen believes he or she is a stakeholder in the state, not a subject of its government.

Partly as a result, they also care about security. Citizens know that their countries have secrets and interests, and want them to be defended vigorously. When these countries catch spies, they prosecute them, rather than hush things up. Some fight wars a lot (America); others not for centuries (Sweden). But they believe in self-defense. They are not pacifists.

Of course other countries fit these descriptions too (the Netherlands, for example) but perhaps not quite so neatly. Because proximity to Russia concentrates minds, the USNB9 have proved less susceptible to Russian influence peddling. Their energy industries have steered clear of the sweetheart deals that have entrapped gas companies in Germany and the Netherlands. Their banks do not habitually launder dirty money from the East. Those shared values are all the more important at a time when the traditional bastions of European and Euro-Atlantic cooperation are weakening. NATO is hollowing out. It remains the world's mightiest military alliance, but around a dozen of its European members show no serious interest in its obligations. America is explicitly refocusing its attention to the western Pacific, as it grapples with a rising China. That does not mean that America is abandoning Europe, but it does need to prioritize its commitments. European solidarity is fraying too. The common European security and defense policy is a fascinating exercise in diplomatic nuance. It has a few practical results in the Western Balkans and in anti-piracy missions off East Africa. But the return on the effort expended is pitiful.

These troubling trends are cause for innovation, not gloom. It is easy to decry "ad hoc" solutions. But the comforting world of the past, like the rosy dreams of the future, is gone. NATO will never return as the one-size-fits-all security arrangement for every European member country. Sweden and Finland will never return to the sidelines under the banner of non-alignment or neutrality. The EU is not going to become a super-state that looks after all its members' external worries. What we have to do now is fit our means to our aims.

The first task—hard security—is the most complex diplomatically. Put at its bluntest, it is to deter any Russian government (including one nastier and madder than this one) to invade the Baltic states. It also involves countering other forms of Russian pressure such as espionage, energy blockades, and psychological warfare. That transcends NATO, but must be centered on it.

The biggest deterrent is American military might, including its nuclear arsenal. NATO allies expect that America would regard a military attack on the Baltic states as a *casus belli*. That remains hugely important. The Baltic states, along with Denmark, are right to be cautious about any security arrangements that might imply that Article 5 and the nuclear guarantee is out of date or weakened.

But caution does not mean paranoia. The Obama administration has done a lot to allay any such fears. It pushed through the NATO contingency plans (more accurately, reinforcement plans) that make it clear that heightened tension in the region would bring a proportionate military response, including a large Polish presence in Lithuania. It has staged reassuring military exercises in the Baltic: Jackal Stone (partly in Lithuania) in 2010 and the regional Amber Hope in 2011. It has also done plenty behind the scenes.

More could be done. An American decision to make Steadfast Jazz in October-November 2013 a really serious exercise would be an appropriate response to Russia's menacing Ladoga and Zapad-09 war games in 2009, which roused justified fears in the Baltics and elsewhere.

But so long as America makes it clear that the Baltic region is part of its irreducible military commitment to Europe, other security cooperation has plenty of scope too. Nordefco (Nordic defence cooperation) has given a public and institutional face to the discreet behind-the-scenes activity that has been going on for years (and in some cases, decades). Nordefco is the right way to deal with one of the most important practical military questions: training for interoperability. An Article 5 guarantee may be seen as the bones, but training and interoperability are the muscle. A body without muscle is a skeleton.

Nordefco sidesteps the irrelevant and distracting question of formal NATO membership for Sweden and Finland. Instead, it provides a mutually beneficial process: the more that Sweden and Finland are involved in NATO and American-led security in the Baltic region, the more secure the region will be. And politicians in Stockholm and Helsinki, by signing up to the EU's solidarity clause, have admitted that their countries' security does not stop at their frontiers.

The most practical example of this kind of desirable cooperation is air policing. Only a few months ago, Baltic officials were vehemently against any non-NATO involvement in the air policing mission (Estonia, Latvia and Lithuania lack their own air forces so their airspace is protected by a rota of NATO allies). Yet on March 27 and 28, Swedish and then Finnish warplanes were involved in a routine air policing exercise involving the shepherding of an "unidentified" plane that had "strayed" into national airspace.[1]

Now that this minor taboo has been broken, it is easy to see how USNB9 cooperation can increase and expand. A financial, human or technical contribution from Sweden and Finland does not lessen the importance of the air policing mission; it enhances it. It underlines an

---

[1] See http://www.nato.int/cps/en/SID-CFE15331-4C114705/natolive/news_85569.htm.

important message to Moscow: these three small countries are not token members of Western clubs—they have real friends who make real commitments to defend them. As well as air policing, other productive areas for cooperation include maritime surveillance, procurement, intelligence, and counter-intelligence.

Two messages are clear from this. First, America needs to maintain reassurance that Nordefco complements, rather than supplements, its role in the Baltic. Secondly, the Baltic states should reflect on their misguided reluctance towards the idea (which luckily did not become too public). Semi-publicly, they insisted that air policing must remain NATO-only because any weakening of it would imply a catastrophic move away from Article 5. That could have easily created a propaganda defeat, once that development occurred. Similarly, it would be a mistake now, in the run-up to the NATO summit in Chicago in May, to brief journalists on the absolute necessity of Steadfast Jazz including a live-fire element (desirable though that would be) and to claim that anything short of that would show a lack of American commitment. Should the live-firing not materialize, then the nay-sayers and doomsters will have a field day. The case of Georgia exemplifies the danger of taking a maximalist position on security demands, in the hope of bluffing America into giving the desired response.

Security has other non-military aspects too. The Swedish banks played a big role in making sure that the Baltic states survived the economic crisis (critics would say that their reckless lending also ensured that the crisis was so bad in the first place). Undersea power cables to Sweden and Finland are helping to end the energy isolation created by the legacy of Soviet planning. Police cooperation helps deal with organized crime. Border guards cooperate on illegal immigration. Behind the scenes the spy-catchers share leads and secrets. Though again, more could be done. It would be good to see a more vehement condemnation of Russian propaganda stunts against the Baltic states, for example.

The second task is the promotion of freedom. Just as old comforting notions are wearing out with regard to security, they are also fraying with regard to politics. The old idea was that the West was on the way to an inexorable triumph because of the innate virtues of its system. That notion has proved to be flawed. One reason is that authoritarian crony capitalism has proved surprisingly resilient. Another is that Western countries have failed to practise what they preach. The friendship between Silvio Berlusconi and Vladimir Putin was no coincidence; each found plenty to admire in the other's political style.

Amid this decay, the USNB9 remain a shop window for good governance. Norway shows that a resource-rich country need not be corrupted by rent-seeking. The Baltic states show countries how to reestablish the rule of law. America shows that it is possible for a big country to be a benign hegemon, not a bullying one. Sweden shows that a former imperial power can have genuinely friendly relations with its former dominions. All the countries, in their different ways, belie the notions peddled by the Kremlin that the West is just like the East, but more successful in disguising it; that only money matters; that talk of human rights and legality is just camouflage, and so on. The USNB9 could do more to polish that shop window and advertise its contents (not only to the East, one might note, but also to the South).

Active politics has a role too. The Russian opposition does not need money (and giving it to those who seek it may do more harm than good). What it really wants is a tougher stance to the regime that is looting Russia and murdering its opponents. This means diplomatic distance: shunning phony initiatives for "joint security" and the like. The Russian regime interprets friendliness as weakness and reacts accordingly. Instead, the approach should center on visa bans and on freezing assets. An excellent start would be for the USNB9 jointly to implement the Magnitsky list visa sanctions (Sergei Magnitsky was a lawyer who died in prison after he uncovered a 230 million dollar fraud against the Russian state, perpetrated by officials. Campaigners on his behalf want 60 beneficiaries of that crime and accomplices in it banned from coming to the West). Similarly, the USNB9 should instigate money-laundering investigations against those who have enriched themselves through bribe-taking and theft and then seek to launder the proceeds in the Western financial system. Many countries agree that these steps are necessary. But nobody wants to be the first to move. The USNB9 is a good forum for agreeing this sort of collective action.

These steps should not apply only to Russia. The USNB9 are well-placed to help the people of Belarus too, with a mixture of targeted sanctions at the top, and broad and generous help at the bottom on issues such as visas, legal aid and media.

As with promoting freedom in Russia, these efforts would not exclude others. Involving the Visegrad countries (the Czech Republic, Hungary, Poland, and Slovakia) would be good (though Poland's self-interested foreign policy towards Russia leaves only modest room for cooperation). Britain would be a welcome ally too (David Cameron has initiated British summits with the Nordic-Baltic eight, though so far without a hard-edged political agenda). But above all the USNB9 offer a unique mixture of focus, flexibility, proximity and clout. Their time is now.

Section II

Embedding and Integration

Chapter Five

The Nordic-Baltic Region: A Cluster of Innovation for Military Cooperation in Europe?

Jānis Sārts

In the modern world where a state's security has increasingly global dimensions and sources of threat are not necessarily from neighboring countries, but might come from a very distant region, individual national military capabilities are insufficient to meet all of their challenges. Therefore we are seeing more and more common international military action instead of individual national application of military power. This has been a growing trend in Europe and in the transatlantic security space for some time. European countries are, more and more, parting with their individual ability to employ military power and are replacing it with cooperative mechanisms that allow fairly effective use of multinational forces. This, and the need, despite the limited sizes and populations of its countries, to keep up with the development of military technology, has led to the profound development of cooperation processes in Europe. In this article, I will try to identify the decisive factors for the success as well as some ways forward for military and defense integration processes based on the lessons learned from military cooperation in the Baltic and Nordic regions and in Europe as a whole.

Real military cooperation is not an easy solution. It takes a lot of adaptation, narrows purely national military options, and requires reliance on others. Sometimes it also means a clumsy decision-making process when all cooperating nations have to agree to employ the joint military capability. Considering these and many other difficulties, why is it important to cooperate and integrate militarily?

Jānis Sārts is State Secretary of the Ministry of Defence of Latvia.

Existing Military Realities

Europe's lack of defense capabilities has long been the theme of serious debate on transatlantic security. Already low defense spending levels in Europe have been hit in recent years by government austerity packages cutting further into the European defense capability. The recently signed EU fiscal stability treaty, with its target of 0.5% governmental structural deficit and for total deficit levels to go below 60% of GDP, undoubtedly means even further tightening of resources and consequently of defense spending. On the other hand, more and more European countries are faced with an inability to ensure military capabilities across the whole spectrum: air, sea, and land. If this trend continues, the future for Europe could hold more fragmented capabilities and bigger holes in military spending. In the situation where Europeans are already unnecessarily duplicating basic elements of the military while under-investing in capabilities that determine the success of the military operation in the 21st century, it is even more worrisome. As a result Europe could face steady military decline resulting in military irrelevance and a loss of international influence. But, due to national limitations, is the only option for the world's biggest economy to become a military puzzle consisting of many small military pieces with the same imprint, but without the ability to produce one big strong picture? This is not necessarily so. Cooperation can help to avoid a large number of the problems described above. The recent crises can in fact pose an opportunity. Under the pressure of austerity, irrational and shortsighted obstacles for military cooperation can be removed. Already in the different regions of Europe we see different forms of cooperative patterns existing and developing. For instance, the BENELUX region, Visegrad countries, Nordic and Baltic cooperation, and even the United Kingdom and France, have come up with interesting and substantive cooperation plans. But these cooperative efforts have, so far, not been enough to improve the situation, more is necessary. Certainly some of the regional examples and solutions can provide ideas for wider and more ambitious European military integration.

There is one region where these processes are at a more advanced stage of integration. Baltic and Nordic states are well known for the success of their cooperation in the military area and their readiness to develop and introduce new cooperative concepts. So what are the factors that make Baltic and Nordic states' cooperation so successful?

Evolution of the Baltic Military Cooperation

When you look at the history of the region it is as complex as one can expect in Europe. As with many regions of the continent, the history of the Baltic and Nordic states contains a multitude of rivalries, long periods of neighborly wars, and different countries expanding their territories throughout the region then fading, afterwards, into the European backyard. We see big European powers playing out their conflicts in this area, some of it taking place in the not-too-distant past. In other words, the region's historical conundrum is as complex and multifaceted as in other parts of the continent. Yet, Baltic and Nordic countries have not only avoided mutual clashes for hundreds of years, they have become one of the most dynamic cooperative regions in Europe overcoming both barriers of history and language, as well as different institutional memberships.

After the collapse of the Soviet system in Europe, the three Baltic states emerged as one of the few Eastern European regions without the inherited Soviet military system. Everything had to be built from scratch: systems, personnel competence, and military capabilities. This created an excellent background for potential cooperation. Starting with 1994 when the first joint Baltic unit (Baltic peacekeeping battalion) was created, the cooperation projects blossomed: BALTRON (joint naval squadron), BALTNET (air surveillance system), BALT-DEFCOL (military college for the middle and senior ranking military personnel) were the biggest and most prominent projects, and there were many others. Those projects were largely created to channel the assistance of other countries' militaries in building Baltic capabilities in the most effective way. However, when support programs finished, most of these projects stayed on and not only provided joint capabilities, but also created an environment conducive to cooperative approaches amongst the military and political leadership. In other words, it developed the habit of cooperation. Not all of the original cooperation projects have survived to this date; some have transformed and some have ended, while others live on providing practical capability. Clearly this outlines that only the projects that really contributed to the capability development and produced cumulative effect of cooperation stood the test of time, while the projects whose primary purpose were competency development lost their raison d'etre and disappeared.

The other outcome of the 20 years of Baltic military cooperation is the acceptance of the necessity to share part of the sovereign decision making with cooperation partners. The ability to accept this on a political level is remarkable and has allowed Baltic nations to adopt necessary rational solutions. One case in point is the Baltic air policing solution. Here Baltic states have agreed not to develop national air interception capabilities in order to ensure air policing, as the total costs of the acquisition and maintenance of this would come at the expense of other military capabilities that are useful in NATO and EU operations, while the total number of fighter planes in Europe already significantly exceeds the common requirement. On the other hand, the cost of having other NATO members' planes in the Baltic airspace means that many elements of normally national decisions are transferred to NATO command, like the decision to shoot down an airplane or what to do with the renegade plane.

Not everything in the Baltic military cooperation could be described as a forward-moving process. Despite many successes there are areas of unrealized possibilities. There have been only a few joint procurement programs resulting in only a small number of logistic cooperation areas. The usual problems of different investment priorities, varying timelines and diverse views on the specific requirements for the equipment have prevented significant progress in these areas. The habit of cooperation has proved not to be strong enough to overcome such problems.

Nordic and Baltic Cooperation

A new element of the cooperative picture in the region is Nordic-Baltic cooperation. After the reinvigoration of the Nordic military cooperation in November 2009 with the signature of the Memorandum of Understanding on defense cooperation a new angle has appeared. Instead of sets of multilateral cooperation of different geometries, the possibility of inter-regional cooperation is emerging.

So far it has been mostly a concept for the future, since both Nordic and Baltic countries are still enhancing their internal cooperative processes. Nevertheless the first step has been taken, when in 2011 Nordic cooperation in three minor areas was extended to the Baltic states and back-to-back military meetings between the militaries of the Nordic and Baltic states commenced. Of course these are only the first steps in a promising endeavor that can bring added military value to the contribution of the Nordic–Baltic states to the security of Europe. Existing operational patterns are also developing where the countries from the Nordic and Baltic cooperation area tend to have joint units in the operations (Latvia-Norway) or working in the same regions (Denmark–Estonia), and are producing joint rapid reaction forces for EU and NATO (Nordic battle group).

The first test to the far-reaching success of this cooperation will be the ability to deliver common procurement programs. The challenges are manifold. First, Nordic states and their different levels of national defense industries have to integrate in a mutually-satisfactory manner. Second, this industry will have to come up with solutions that are cost effective, efficient, and adequate, to interest the Baltic states, which, without their own industries, have been accustomed to buying military equipment unlimited by national industrial constrains. Third, for long-lasting results this solution will have to consider Baltic industrial interests that governments will be intent on following when investing considerable national resources into the procurement projects. Consistent, rather than sporadic, multinational procurement is one of the litmus tests of deep military cooperation and integration.

Effects of Ongoing Operations Regarding Military Integration

There is also the factor of operational engagement that has an influence on cooperative patterns. Looking at the example of the ISAF operation in Afghanistan, smaller nations tend to participate alongside other nations. Two solutions are possible: one, when the small nation is integrated under a bigger nation; the other example, when a number of smaller nations come together to produce common capability. Both examples in different ways foster cooperation, beyond immediate effect of the operational impact. Latvia's military has had the opportunity to test both solutions and these have had a positive effect on our military capabilities that has spanned beyond the limits of the ISAF operation and provided longer lasting impacts.

One was the example of the joint Latvia-U.S. OMLT (Operational Mentoring and Liaison Team) in Eastern Afghanistan. This unit that mentored an Afghan battalion was Latvian-led, supported by Michigan National Guard and integrated into the U.S. chain of command. Operationally, it produced an added effect by combining experienced professional military from Latvia (each having experience of at least three operational tours in Iraq and Afghanistan) with the resources and technology heavily provided by the U.S. At the same time, from the perspective of Latvian enabling capabilities, it jumpstarted Latvia's JTAC (joint terminal attack controller) capability that now allows Latvian certified soldiers to direct U.S. airpower. Normally for the Latvian military, which has no air strike capability, it would be impossible to achieve this highly essential capability, but its practical operational requirement and the operational necessity has allowed us not only to possess this capability, but also to develop it at a level that enables Latvia to instruct and help to improve similar capabilities in other smaller NATO countries.

The other example is Latvia's cooperation with Norway in Afghanistan. In the Provincial Reconstruction Team in Meymaneh, Norwegians and Latvians jointly provide functional support for the local Afghan authorities providing in equal measure civil development assistance and military security. As a result of this cooperation we have created integrated lines of logistics, synchronized military procedures and other elements that ensure survival and effectiveness in critical situations. Operational realities, by demonstrating the need for effective logistic supply lines and maintenance, have subtly introduced increased synchronization of military equipment between Latvia and Norway. We see that more than six years of a joint participation of Latvia and Norway in the Afghanistan operation has resulted in an increased level of integration of militaries even without separate political processes and cooperative development programs. This would substantiate the argument that integrated units of smaller and medium sized nations in military operations contributed to the overall process of defense integration. Of course, the smaller the size of units that are integrated, the bigger the integration difficulties. It requires a more significant level of personnel preparation: language, procedures, habits etc. Therefore such units should not be established for only short periods of time. The positive effects of this could only outweigh the difficulties and pains of the establishment if conducted over a longer time period. Soldiers, commanders and commands, both in field and back home, take time to adapt. However, once this happens, the effects spread deeper into the military structures and into the individual knowledge of the soldiers and officers.

European Defense Cooperation Patterns

In Europe the cooperative patterns can be divided into two major groups. First, when all countries come together to create a capability that most of them cannot produce and sustain on their own (Alliance Ground Surveillance), but are essential for their collective operational success. The other level is when a smaller group of countries, normally regionally-based, build on efficiencies of distance and cultural understanding and create integrated capabilities to enhance the sum of their combined individual capabilities.

The development of both will be essential for the future of transatlantic capability cohesion, and the European ability to remain a partner of the U.S. in military operations. The ability of the more militarily potent countries to accept the integrative approach that requires political admission of the limits of applying military power individually and also, at the end of the day, the loss of certain elements of traditional national sovereignty will be crucial. The example of NATO's ability to employ its AWACS (Airborne Warning and Control System) capability during the Libya campaign, or the limits of it because of the reservations of one ally to use its military personnel in this specific mission, illuminates some of the challenges that are inherent in such cooperative approaches. For future joint military capabilities, safeguarding mechanisms should be built in to avoid situations when particular reservations of one participating nation ruins the ability of the other nations to employ these capabilities, if they so require. It once again demonstrates that cooperation is more than just the issue of technical interoperability of troops, procedural similarities or the ability to speak the same language. To a large extent it is the cooperation mindset of the practitioners, of the leadership, but also the ability and readiness to accept both the advantages and the limits and responsibilities imposed on individual national decision making.

The other level of cooperation that relates to the groups of smaller countries normally has a regional context. In this framework the need and ability of military cooperation is much wider. The main engine of regional cooperation is the necessity to produce the most effective solutions not only for the out-of-area operations, but also for national security and defense solutions. There is significant potential for improved efficiency in combining elements of educational systems within the regions, coordinated development of the training capacities of the military units as well as a more integrated approach to the surveillance and control of sea and air space. The Baltic model of the joint air surveillance system with one air control center and NATO's air policing solution for the region are two examples of efficient and bold solutions. Simultaneously, the necessity to produce self-sustainable units in far away operations, like Afghanistan, shows the need for cooperation in producing bigger units, developing integrated logistics, supply lines, and joint maintenance and to drive down the cost for the deployment and sustainment of the national contribution. That in turn allows for the synchronization of the requirements for defense equipment and further rapprochement between defense industries.

Enablers of the Success of Military Cooperation

Examining different angles of cooperation in the military field, there are some common elements that characterize successful cooperative projects. Put simply, these are the enablers of successful defense cooperation. Let us assess some such elements that arose while analyzing the cooperation experience of Latvia and regional cooperation in Europe.

- The first effect that has already come out in the previous elements is the *culture of cooperation*. That is to say that not only the policymakers and implementers have a culture of cooperation, but also people, who would have to deliver within the units, headquarters and agencies understand, accept and possess the habit of cooperation. For the organizations it is important that there is knowledge of how to cope with this external factor in everyday situations practically, legally and procedurally.

- *Compatible* results of the *military education systems* are also a key factor of the success. The ability to interact major to major from different educational systems and expect that the amount of knowledge, experience and ability would allow for equal interaction. The joint military educational establishments have a far reaching impact on the cooperation potential of the countries involved. Also, educational exchange programs, although not as effective, can help improve the culture of cooperation.

- One factor that cannot be overestimated is the ability to communicate freely in the same *language* not only at senior levels but also for junior officers, NCOs and soldiers. It is no coincidence that the most successful cooperative regions in Europe are those where citizens are able to speak in the same language at a fluent level. For both Nordic and Baltic countries, due to the size of their populations, English has become a must for every professional, thus enhancing overall language skills and improving the ability to speak freely in the same language.

- Political *acceptance of the sacrifices* necessary to have an effective cooperation is another must. There is a difference between a political declaration on the need to cooperate and the true political dedication to it. Without that, it is impossible to make tough, from the national perspective, political decisions that make true cooperation possible. Giving up certain industrial interests, accepting limits to national sovereign decisions, being ready for the wider operational interest withstanding national political pressures are only a few examples of the many sacrifices needed.

- The defense industry undeniably has a large potential influence on defense integration. In fact it is one of the prerequisites for success. *Defense industries cooperation* and integration is required for a successful joint procurement, that in turn is the basis for the creation of coordinated, cost-saving logistical and maintenance systems for the military.

- A truly successful cooperation always has a *long-term perspective*. Although there are usually projects that have a limited perspective, these are not the ones that thrive over longer time periods. But the cooperation that results in the capabilities that respond to long-lasting requirements are normally the ones that survive and have a positive effect on overall cooperative patterns.

- The last important success factor is that there should be *no cooperation for cooperation's sake*. All cooperative projects have to lead to a practical result. And it has to offer an outcome that is of higher quality, offers larger benefits and is more rational than the potential national solution.

This is not an exhaustive list of all the essential factors for successful defense cooperation, but one that has derived from the successes and failures of the military cooperation patterns in the Nordic-Baltic region.

A Decade from Now

If this military cooperation behavior existing in the Nordic-Baltic region and other parts of Europe is to continue, in a decade one will see a significant rise in integrated militaries. Nations will have started the introduction of a larger number of common defense platforms, but some capabilities will still be linked to purely national choice and logic. Nordic and Baltic countries will be able to field larger integrated units for their operations or have rapid reaction forces and the ability to deploy and sustain them over distances, which will be more effective and cost efficient. Education of middle and senior ranking officers will be more interrelated and a larger proportion of the education will be conducted in the English language. Much more cooperation will arise in the Baltic Sea region in the maritime area, with more joint capabilities and air defense solutions also becoming more integrated. This is a vision of the future that of course does not take into consideration major global security shifts or major developments in the areas adjacent to the Baltic Sea region that can alter significantly the current processes. But certainly this region is innovative in its approach to cooperation and readiness to integrate, and will continue to be as such, with the added cumulative effect of the experiences amassed that will serve as one of the examples in the process of synchronization of European military capabilities. In Europe the financial realities of the next decade and the security realities will raise existential questions that will lead to more rapid integration processes both for the military and for the defense industries. And, I am sure, as was the case many times before, our democratic societies will prove their resilience and ability to rise to the challenge and neither Europe nor our transatlantic community will become irrelevant, but instead will become a model of persistence and adaptation.

Chapter Six

Defense Integration in the Baltic Sea Security Complex—A Conceptual Approach

Mike Winnerstig

The Baltic Sea area, i.e. Scandinavia, the Baltic States, Poland, Germany, and the westernmost parts of Russia, is not an area that is currently associated with military conflicts. On the contrary, since the mid-1990s it has been a remarkably peaceful part of the world. At the same time, there have been and still are several signs indicating that tensions among some of the countries of the area do exist, and that some of those tensions might be rising. The purpose of the following text is, first, to explore conceptually how the Baltic Sea area might be analyzed, and second, to identify ways in which its peaceful character can be maintained and enhanced.

The Baltic Sea Area as a Security Complex

From a security policy perspective, the Baltic Sea area can be defined in several ways. Most of the countries involved—with the exceptions of Norway and Russia—are members of the European Union, which is an *inter-* and partly *supra*national organization. The scope of EU integration is very wide, and EU-related transnational cooperation takes place in most areas of politics. Most of the Baltic Sea countries—with the exceptions of Sweden, Finland, and Russia—are also members of NATO, which is a strictly *inter*national political-military alliance organization. The importance of NATO for the whole transatlantic security area—including Canada and the U.S.—

Dr. Mike Winnerstig is a deputy director of research at the Swedish Defence Research Agency (FOI) and a member of the Royal Swedish Academy of the War Sciences. The views presented in this article are strictly his own and do not in any way represent the views of the FOI, the Swedish Ministry of Defence or the Swedish Government.

and for the military integration of its members' armed forces can hardly be overstated.

Thus, it could be argued that the Baltic Sea area is also currently a very well integrated area when it comes to military security. According to many theorists of international relations, this means that wars are highly unlikely; the processes of integration—both within the EU and NATO—function in such a way that tensions between countries are not allowed to grow to military conflicts. The peaceful effects of increased integration are also frequently mentioned in solemn speeches by political leaders of the area.

But it is also possible to see the Baltic Sea area in another way. During the Cold War, the Baltic Sea area was a border country between East (the Soviet Union and the Warsaw Pact) and the West (the United States and the rest of the NATO countries). Finland was not part of any military alliance but was—through the so-called Agreement of Friendship, Cooperation, and Mutual Assistance with the Soviet Union—associated with the latter country. Sweden was not a member of any military alliance either, although contemporary research shows that the Swedish military and security policy-related linkages with the West and NATO (especially the U.S. and the UK) were much stronger than was publicly known during the Cold War.[1]

During the Cold War, however, it was perfectly possible for both Sweden and Finland to argue officially—not least by references to the so-called policy of neutrality—that the interactions or conflicts of other countries in the Baltic Sea area did not affect them. The stated goal of Swedish security policy for most of the Cold War was explicitly to keep Sweden out of any conflicts in its own neighborhood. Accordingly, it could be argued that the Baltic Sea area during the Cold War was little more than a general extension of the geopolitics of the Cold War itself, with Sweden and Finland acting as buffer zones between the two military blocs in Europe.

---

[1] See, for two excellent recent examples of this, Robert Dalsjö (2007): *Life-line Lost. The Rise and Fall of "Neutral" Sweden's Secret Reserve Option of Wartime Help from the West* (Stockholm: Santérus); and Mikael Holmström (2011): *Den dolda alliansen: Sveriges hemliga NATO-förbindelser* [The Hidden Alliance: Sweden's Secret NATO Linkages] (Stockholm: Atlantis).

Today, some 20 years after the end of the Cold War, the situation has changed fundamentally. Interactions in the Baltic Sea area abound; economic and political linkages develop at high speed; business relationships that were completely impossible, even unthinkable during the Cold War—such as the extraordinarily big role that Swedish banks currently play in all the three Baltic economies—all have transformed the situation. The area of defense is, admittedly, much less developed than the economic sphere, but with the integration of the Baltic states into NATO in 2004, more than half of Scandinavia is now also militarily allied with their Baltic neighbors. Military issues, however, are also those—though not only those—that have generated considerable friction between Russia on the one side and the NATO allies of the area on the other during the last few years. The NATO plans for missile defense installations in Poland and the quite undiplomatic Russian military exercises of *Zapad* and *Ladoga* 2009 are issues that have led to a considerable amount of verbal tension, at the very least.[2]

Thus, rather than considering the Baltic Sea area to be a profoundly peaceful place, governed by the domesticating effects of political integration, one might be forced to accept that it does contain seeds of potential conflict. Therefore, it could be more fruitful to regard it as what the British international relations theorist Barry Buzan has labeled a "security complex," i.e. a group of states "whose primary security concerns link together sufficiently closely that their national securities cannot realistically be considered apart from one another."[3] According to Buzan, a security complex often contains a number of states of markedly varying power bases—i.e. essentially both small and big states—and their local issues and relations have a dominant role in defining the national security priorities of each state within the complex. The issues involved can be of both domestic and inter-state char-

---

[2] On the missile defense issue, see for example Anders Lennartsson & Fredrik Lindvall (2011): *USAs bidrag till Natos missilförsvar [The US Contribution to the NATO Missile Defence System]*, FOI-R—3226—SE (Stockholm: FOI Defence Analysis]. On the Russian exercises, see e.g. Roger McDermott (2009), "Zapad 2009 Rehearses Countering a NATO Attack on Belarus," Jamestown Foundation, http://www.jamestown.org/single/?no_cache=1&tx_ttnews%5Btt_news%5D=35558.

[3] Barry Buzan (1983): *People, States and Fear: The National Security Problem in International Relations* (Worcester: Wheatsheaf Books), pp. 105f.

acter, and they also define the principal binding insecurities—i.e. the bases of possible conflict—of the complex as a whole.[4]

To Buzan, a security complex offers an approach to security which deals both with the macro-level of international relations of the states involved and the micro-level of their local issues, such as ethnic groups of one state living within the borders of another. In taking this approach, Buzan noted that security complexes can lead to "external influences tending to amplify local problems, and local problems shaping and constraining external entanglements and influences."[5]

Buzan introduced this concept almost 30 years ago, at which time his own pet example of a security complex was south Asia, a corner of the world very different from the Baltic Sea area. Despite this, the security complex notion is not only theoretically appealing, but also of potentially practical importance when it comes to dealing with the actual security problems of the Baltic Sea countries and their surrounding neighbors. A lot of the current political issues of the area— such as ethnic minorities in the Baltic states, the military relationship between Sweden and NATO, and the general thrust of Russian foreign policy toward its Western neighbors—can be contained within the framework of a security policy complex; the issues might have local roots, but they affect all parties of the complex and they tend to survive as long as the complex as a whole does not transform into something else.

On the latter issue, concerning the transformation of a security complex, Buzan devised essentially three models. In the first place, a security complex could be overtaken by another, larger, and/or global setting. This was essentially the case of the Baltic Sea area during the Cold War. Secondly, the basic rivalries or inter-state problems could be obliterated by force, i.e. if a stronger part conquers or destroys its adversaries within the complex. This is a far-fetched scenario in the current world of Baltic Sea security since it would entail a full-fledged war between, say, Russia and the entire Western world. The third model of eventual evolution of a security complex is, according to Buzan, its transformation into a *security community*. A security commu-

---

[4] Ibid. pp. 106f.

[5] Ibid. p. 112.

nity "exists among independent states which do not expect or fear the use of force in relations between them."[6] By extension, this should—or at least could—also entail a conception of shared threats and shared responses to these threats, military or otherwise.

Buzan exemplified the security community concept with the relations between Canada and the U.S., but it is clear that the same kind of relations today define the relations between the Nordic and Baltic states, respectively, as well; security communities are "resolved or matured security complexes in which basic conflicts have been worked out."[7] This applies, for instance, to the Nordic states taken in isolation but certainly not for the Baltic Sea area as a whole. From a practitioner's perspective, on the other hand, transforming this whole area to such a security community might be a highly desirable end-goal of statesmanship.

So, if we consider the current Baltic Sea area as a security complex, what practical implications does this have for the policies of the states involved? In the first place, this means that in contrast to the Cold War era, the security policy situation of, for example, Sweden is highly integrated with—and dependent on—not only the security situation of Finland, but also that of the Baltic states, Poland, Germany, and Russia. This is in principle nothing new for long-time NATO allies such as Denmark and Norway, but it is certainly a new situation for the post-neutral countries of Sweden and Finland—at least in conceptual terms.

Furthermore, considering Buzan's line of reasoning, the security complex notion merits an investigation of the area's conflict potential, also in terms of factors that are untraditional from a security policy perspective but which might appear as sources of conflict. The latter includes not only ethnic minority issues but also cyber security and energy security, together with various economic factors that can promote both conflict and cooperation.

For the purposes of this fairly brief paper, I will focus on whether the field of defense cooperation between the Nordic-Baltic countries (the NB8) seems to be consistent with the optimistic interpretation of

---

[6] Ibid. pp. 114f.

[7] Ibid. p. 115.

the security complex notion, i.e. whether it seems to be directed toward increased integration, which eventually might constitute a cornerstone in the making of a fully-fledged security community of the Baltic Sea area as a whole.

Nordic-Baltic Defense Cooperation and the NB8 Concept

The Current Security Policies of the NB8

The Nordic-Baltic Eight (NB8) is actually a fairly old concept. In the 1990s, after the process of Baltic independence, the eight countries began meeting with each other at different levels, but for many years the activities were primarily organized by their foreign ministries and the issues dealt with did not directly include defense issues.

Today there is a certain paradox when it comes to the Nordic countries and their current security and defense policies; although these five countries are often regarded as very similar, in terms of politics as well as concerning cultural and societal issues, none of them conducts a security policy identical to any other Nordic country. Iceland is a member of NATO but not of the EU, and has no defense forces of its own. Norway shares the same membership situation but does have a considerable defense force, closely linked to the U.S. and the UK, especially in its naval aspects. Denmark is a member of both NATO and the EU, but entertains an opt-out both when it comes to the EU's fledgling defense dimension and the euro. Sweden is a member of the EU—and highly active in the EU's defense activities—but has rejected adopting the euro, and is not a member of NATO. Finland is a member of the EU and has adopted the euro, making the country in principle more EU-integrated than Sweden, but is likewise not a NATO member.

In contrast to this Nordic heterogeneity in defense integration, the Baltic states are strikingly homogeneous: all of them are members of both NATO and the EU, and although only Estonia has so far adopted the euro, both Latvia and Lithuania also strive toward this change. It is therefore fair to say that all the Baltic countries are already more integrated in the general Euro-Atlantic security framework than any of their Nordic neighbors. It is worthwhile to keep these relationships in mind when considering the future of NB8 defense integration.

The Development of NB8 Defense Cooperation

As noted above, the Baltic states are—at least after 2004—in principle the most integrated in the major international security-related organizations, such as NATO and the EU. However, given their size, and the fact that issues of territorial defense were highly unpopular within NATO before the Russo-Georgian war of 2008, the practical implications of this might have been less than the Baltic states had hoped for—at least until 2010. During this year, according to press reports, official statements and the Wikileaks revelations, fully-fledged plans for the territorial defense of the Baltic states were adopted by NATO.[8] Although there are some question marks about the practical implications of these plans given the cutbacks of military troops in NATO Europe, their existence implies that the Baltic states are clearly integrated militarily with their Nordic allies in the NATO framework.

However, on the Nordic side—the heterogeneous part of the NB8—several attempts have been made in order to increase cooperation in the defense field. The so-called Stoltenberg report, published in 2009 and written by the former Norwegian minister of foreign affairs, Thorvald Stoltenberg, presented a number of concrete proposals on how to increase both foreign and security policy cooperation among the Nordic states—including a kind of mutual defense guarantee between the five states.[9] Partly because of the latter proposal, the Stoltenberg report never made it that far in the public discourse of the countries involved.

During the same year, however, several other important events started to frame the whole issue of defense in the Nordic states. The

---

[8] See, for example, Bo Ljung, Tomas Malmlöf, Karlis Neretnieks & Mike Winnerstig (forthcoming 2012): *The Security and Defensibility of the Baltic States—a Comprehensive Analysis* (Stockholm: FOI Defence Analysis), esp. chapters 3 and 4.

[9] See Thorvald Stoltenberg (2009): Nordic Cooperation On Foreign and Security Policy: Proposals presented to the extraordinary meeting of Nordic foreign ministers in Oslo on 9 February 2009, http://www.regeringen.se/content/1/c6/12/01/83/94662 dc3.pdf.

EU's Lisbon Treaty was adopted, and with it two kinds of mutual assistance clauses; in the first place a solidarity clause relating to mutual assistance in the event of a terrorist attack, a natural disaster or the like in a member state (art. 2.2.2), second was a traditional defense assistance clause of the NATO art. 5 variety (art. 42.7). However, as it was established in the treaty that for the EU members which are also NATO members, NATO arrangements in terms of defense are those which will be followed by these members, the notion of the EU as a military alliance fell short pretty quickly. It initiated, however, a discussion on defense and solidarity in both Sweden and Finland.

Partly as a result of this, the Swedish Parliament adopted a major defense bill in the summer of 2009. In this bill, two major changes of Swedish security policy were introduced. Firstly, the government stated—in fundamental contrast to the Swedish security policy doctrine's main tenets since the early 19th century—that Sweden will not remain passive if a disaster or an attack should afflict another EU member state or Nordic country, and that Sweden also expects these countries to act in the same manner if Sweden is affected. Secondly, in order to operationalize this, the government tasked the Swedish armed forces to be able both to give and to receive military assistance.[10] Both these issues—being affected by attacks on other states and being able to help them militarily as well as receiving help from them in the event of an attack on Sweden—had been, with minor exceptions, anathema for Swedish security policy decision-makers since 1812. A peculiarity of this new doctrine—labeled the "solidarity declaration" in Sweden—is its unilateral character; in announcing it, Sweden did not ask for any reciprocity but instead seemed to rely on "expectations," i.e. that other countries would come to Sweden's assistance without any prior official endorsement of this doctrine—and vice versa. The new doctrine led to a few public critical comments in Sweden, especially by theologists of the traditional neutrality policy,[11] but was in general accepted without much fanfare—

---

[10]Ministry of Defence (2009), *A Useful Defence*, The Swedish Government's Bill 2008/09:140, esp. p. 9. See http://www.regeringen.se/content/1/c6/12/29/57/853ca644.pdf.

[11]See, for example, Mikael Nilsson (2009), "Ny doktrin sätter freden på spel" [New Doctrine Puts Peace at Risk], *Svenska Dagbladet*, Dec. 2, http://www.svd.se/opinion/brannpunkt/ny-doktrin-satter-freden-pa-spel_3878379.svd.

and, one could add, much public knowledge of the doctrinal change. As the bill also contained the framework for a major defense reform, including making conscription "dormant" and forming instead a small, all-volunteer force of about ten percent of the manpower available during the Cold War, its contents were actually quite revolutionary.[12]

In Finland, the other "odd man out" country in terms of military alliance membership among the NB8, no identical doctrine was adopted, although Finland officially and strongly adhered to the solidarity and defense clauses of the EU Lisbon Treaty.

Also during 2009, fledgling Nordic cooperation on defense materiel and related issues—which had been going on in an ad hoc fashion for many years—took on a more institutionalized character through the establishment of NORDEFCO (Nordic Defence Co-Operation.) The primary driver for this cooperation was economic issues—such as making better use of decreasing defense budgets through common materiel purchases and the like—and it was publicly stated that the framework as such had no purpose of building new forms of military alliances.[13]

In 2010, a potential milestone in NB8 cooperation was reached, through the publication of a report of two "wise men," the former Latvian Prime Minister and Foreign Minister Valdis Birkavs, representing the Baltic countries, and the former Danish Minister of Defense Søren Gade, representing the Nordic countries. The report was comprehensive, but in the field of defense cooperation its main recommendations stayed within the realms of the politically non-dangerous, such as encouraging all the NB8 countries to contribute to the EU Nordic Battle Group of 2011 and recommending the Nordic countries to further strengthen the Baltic Defence College in Tartu,

---

[12]The Royal Swedish Academy of the War Sciences published a major study on the solidarity declaration in 2011, which was published in English the year after. This volume contained among other things some critical analyses of the practical abilities to sustain militarily the implicit promises of the solidarity declaration, but has so far not achieved a lot of public attention. See Bo Hugemark [ed.] (2012): *Friends in Need: Towards a Swedish Strategy of Solidarity with her Neighbours* (Stockholm: Royal Academy of the War Sciences).

[13]See http://www.nordefco.org/facts-about-nordefco/.

Estonia (BDC).[14] The BDC is a joint Baltic defense academy supported financially by, among others, the Nordic countries.

What the Wise Men report did do, however, was discuss strategically the "branding" of the NB8 concept, as it noted that "key stakeholders and ordinary citizens do not seem to have sufficient knowledge of NB8 cooperation" and that more could be done in terms of public diplomacy.[15]

That more was going on in the defense field of the NB8 cooperation became apparent—at least at an expert level, if not at the level of public opinion—in 2011, when the Baltic states were invited by the then Swedish chairmanship to join some of the NORDEFCO cooperation areas.[16] The issues—advanced distributed learning (ADL), the Nordic Centre for Gender in Operations and veteran issues—were perhaps not the crucial defense issues of the day, but showed that the integration of the NB8 in the defense field had reached another stage. This impression was reinforced in 2012 when the Baltic states for the first time were invited to participate in a meeting of the NORDE-FCO military coordination committee.[17]

However, sensitivities remain among the NB8 countries when it comes to military solidarity (i.e. mutual defense assistance), in contrast to defense materiel cooperation. First of all, this has to do with the fact that six out of the eight countries are already members of NATO, the primary organization for politico-military solidarity and collective defense in Europe, and none of these countries want the NB8 cooperation to become a substitute for NATO. Furthermore, the two post-neutral countries of the NB8, Sweden and Finland, are still affected by the public opinion of their electorates, which have not kept up with the speed of the real developments in terms of Nordic-Baltic defense cooperation.

Examples of these sensitivities include the so-called Nordic solidarity declaration of 2011, which is an agreement among the five Nordic

---

[14]See http://baltikum2011.dk/fileadmin/templates/pdf/NB_8_WiseMen%20Report. pdf, p. 11f.

[15]Ibid. pp. 13f.

[16]http://www.nordefco.org/latest-updates/the-nordic/.

[17]http://www.nordefco.org/latest-updates/the-baltic/.

countries that considered their strong common values and their desire to cooperate on challenges "in the area of foreign and security policy in a spirit of solidarity," but the issues mentioned in the declaration were "natural and man-made disasters, cyber and terrorist attacks." There was a conspicuous absence of military attack as a cause of solidarity.[18]

Another example relates to the NATO exercise CMX 2011, which was a NATO crisis management exercise with territorial defense elements, played out as a staff exercise only but with the scenario geographically situated off the coast of Norway. All 28 NATO nations participated, as did Finland and Sweden as partner countries. The sensitive issue relating to this exercise, from a Finnish and Swedish traditional perspective, was that it made full use of the NATO art. 4 and art. 5 consultation and operational mechanisms.

According to press reports, Norway was the militarily attacked party in the fictional scenario. This led Norway and NATO to ask Sweden for help, including military assistance. After very briefly deliberating the issues involved, Sweden did not only participate as an observing partner country but actually provided substantial military and geopolitical assets in order to help to defend Norway, together with NATO, against the aggressor state of Vineland, an invented island nation west of Norway.[19] This was allegedly done with explicit references to the Swedish security declaration of 2009, and with which the scenario seems to be perfectly in line.

However, probably because of the political sensitivities involved—not least concerning fears of a public opinion backlash—the actions taken within the realm of the exercise have not been discussed publicly by either the government or the parliamentary opposition in Sweden.

Finally, some issues related to what could be called "security policy identity" seem to have increased in importance. In the first place, the

---

[18]See the full text at http://www.formin.fi/Public/default.aspx?contentid=217312.

[19]See Claes Arvidsson (2012): "Sverige krigar ihop med Nato när Norge angrips" (Sweden Fights Together With NATO When Norway is Attacked), *Svenska Dagbladet*, Jan. 15th, http://www.svd.se/opinion/ledarsidan/sverige-krigar-ihop-med-nato-nar-norge-angrips_6770621.svd. See for details on the exercise as such also *CMX 2011*, http://uknato.fco.gov.uk/en/news/?view=News&id=674946482.

Baltic states have tended to underline their relationship with the Nordic countries also in terms of identity discourse. Estonia has had the easiest case in this regard, as the Estonians ethnically and linguistically are closely related to the Finns. Moreover, the long era of Swedish rule over Estonia (1561–1721) is known as the "Golden Swedish Era" in Estonian historical discourse. However, it should also be noted that Lithuania—perhaps the Baltic country least related to the Scandinavian states in terms of culture, religion, and societal issues—has during the last years embarked on a determined effort to redirect itself toward the "Nordics" at least in the sense of a "strategic orientation" toward the Nordic area.[20] The current Lithuanian foreign minister, Audronius Ažubalis, has actually officially framed this in terms that are surprisingly similar to the factors discussed by Buzan in his developing of the security complex concept:

> Just like in the Vasa period, the foreign policies in the North and in the East are directly interdependent, and key political interests of the Baltic, Nordic and Central European countries coincide. The revived historic Nordic partnership presents a great opportunity for Lithuania to even more effectively promote democratic processes and build the well-being in our neighbouring Eastern European countries.[21]

By extension, this would also mean that the Nordic-Baltic states have primary security concerns that link together sufficiently closely so that their national securities cannot realistically be considered separate from one another, to frame it in Buzanesque terms.

---

[20]See "Lithuania's strategic orientation towards the Nordic-Baltic region is based on historical experience, says Foreign Minister," *Lithuania Tribune*, Oct. 19, 2011, http://www.lithuaniatribune.com/2011/10/19/lithuania %E2%80%99s-strategic-orientation-towards-the-nordic-baltic-region-is-based-on-historical-experience-says-foreign-minister/.

[21]Ibid. As a historical footnote, the Vasa period—named after the then Swedish royal family, which ruled Sweden from 1523 to 1654—was a period when Sweden and Lithuania had several very intricate connections, including both wars and royalty, such as Sigismund III—who for a brief period was not only the king of Sweden but simultaneously the king of Poland and the grand duke of Lithuania.

In a related, although not identical, fashion, public statements on Swedish security policy are also proof of what could be called a security policy identity change. For example, when speaking at a major conference on security and defense policy in early 2010, the then-Swedish minister of defense, Sten Tolgfors, argued that the Swedish defense policy had now adopted a "neighborhood perspective":

> The design and orientation of the Swedish armed forces have and will have a clear Baltic Sea profile. The [Swedish] defence policy has now adopted a new neighborhood perspective, whose starting point is that Sweden builds security with others. (...) Security is built together with our neighbors in the Nordic countries and the EU. You cannot see a situation where a threat only affects one of the countries in our region.[22]

Likewise, in the 2012 foreign policy declaration to the Swedish parliament, the minister of foreign affairs, Carl Bildt, stated the following:

> Sweden's security is built in solidarity with others. Threats to peace and security are deterred collectively and in cooperation with other countries and organisations. (...) Sweden will not remain passive if another EU Member State or Nordic country suffers a disaster or an attack. We expect these countries to act in the same way if Sweden is similarly affected. We must be in a position to both give and receive support, civilian and military. (...) Cooperation between Sweden and our Nordic and Baltic neighbours has deep roots. Together, we have achieved peace and freedom throughout our region, and today we can combine our forces to propel these values beyond our own borders.[23]

---

[22]Minister of Defense Sten Tolgfors, (2010), *Försvarsförmåga i fokus—ett försvarspolitiskt paradigmskifte [Defence Capability in Focus: A Defence Policy Paradigm Shift]*, speech at the People and Defence Conference in Sälen, Sweden on January 17, 2010. My translation. See http://www.regeringen.se/sb/d/3214/a/138070.

[23]Minster of Foreign Affairs Carl Bildt, (2012): *Statement of Government Policy in the Parliamentary Debate on Foreign Affairs*, Wednesday, 15 February. See http://www. regeringen.se/content/1/c6/18/62/82/05a76 46d.pdf.

Here it is: the indivisibility of security, the mutuality of defense policy, and the importance of a select number of neighbors; i.e., a security complex. What is also apparent is the complete lack of the old-time, non-aligned, neutrality-oriented isolationism that was part and parcel of Swedish security policy for almost 200 years.

NB8 Defense Cooperation—Some Tentative Conclusions

As can be seen from the narrative above, NB8 cooperation is a growing field, which includes the area of defense. Without doubt, the NB8 countries now recognize—if implicitly—that they are part of the same security complex, i.e. their primary national security concerns cannot be dealt with in national isolation; they are all dependent on each other's security. Thus, the fact that several of these countries, as noted above, frame their security discourses in terms of solidarity is not surprising. However, at the same time, sensitivities and hesitations concerning practical expressions of military solidarity still exist in all the countries involved. One of the reasons for this is the incoherence of the NB8 countries in terms of organizational membership in the EU and NATO, respectively.

It becomes more and more clear, however, that the NB8 concept in itself has transformative capabilities. We see it clearly in the strivings of the Baltic states to go "Nordic." We see it also in the almost revolutionary transformation of Swedish security and defense policy over the last few years, which has been clearly influenced by the concept of neighborhood solidarity—not least relating to the NB8 countries. In Finland, this is also visible but to a much lesser degree—Finnish security and defense policy is also in for major changes, but these seem to be caused by economic factors rather than a fully-fledged transformation of the foundations of the policy itself.[24]

---

[24]See e.g. Bo Ljung and Karlis Neretnieks (2011), *Kommande reformering av den finländska försvarsmakten* [The Future Reforms of the Finnish Armed Forces], FOI Memo 3843 (Stockholm: FOI).

Prospects for Achieving a NB8 Security Community

With this brief summary of NB8 defense cooperation in mind, what can be said about the prospects of the Baltic Sea security complex becoming a security community?

In the first place, it seems to be fair to say that the NB8 countries form a security complex, and not a security community, among themselves. Military conflicts among the NB8 are of course out of the question, but it is not necessarily the case that all of the NB8 countries would support each other militarily should an external attack against one or several of them occur. For example, according to current Finnish doctrine, it is far from certain that Finland would militarily support any of the Baltic states, should they be attacked by an external actor.

However, this setting is slowly changing—as was exemplified by the Swedish case mentioned above—and if certain prerequisites are fulfilled the NB8 countries could constitute a security community quite easily and very quickly. These prerequisites are, however, pretty difficult to obtain.

In the Nordic case, for domestic political reasons, there is reluctance in both Sweden and Finland to joining NATO; the alliance being the most obvious practical expression of politico-military solidarity in the whole transatlantic area. This reluctance effectively obstructs the practical ability of the NB8 to form a true security community. If the defense planning of all the eight states would be performed within an allied NATO framework, almost the whole Baltic Sea area would be covered by one single politico-military structure, which would not only bring the NB8 countries much closer to each other, but would also diminish considerably all forms of military threats to the region. The freedom of maneuver for any aggressor would be extremely limited. Norway's and Iceland's eventual joining the EU would also contribute to this, albeit to a lesser extent.

There are signs, though, that things are changing in this context. Two of the four current Swedish governmental coalition parties—including the Moderate liberal-conservative party of the Prime Minister, the Foreign Minister and the Defense Minister—are openly promoting Swedish NATO membership, whereas the two others are still undecided but on the verge of changing their traditional non-aligned/neutralist position. In Finland, the debate is more geared towards negative stances regarding NATO, but given the current problems of Finnish defense policy this might change as well.

In the NATO member states of Norway and Iceland, public opinion seems to be dead set against EU membership, which—given the EU's difficulties both in the economic and defense spheres—will most likely persist for the foreseeable future. However, since the EU's role in the field of European and Baltic Sea area defense is limited compared to NATO's, this is not necessarily a big problem for the prospect of achieving a security community.

In the Baltic states, the ability of dealing with certain domestic issues relating to Russia—such as energy security and the Russian-speaking minorities of the Baltic states—will also be a clear indicator of whether the Baltic Sea security complex stands any chance of transforming into a security community as a whole. This might also entail a profound reorientation of Russian policy, which could be extremely difficult to achieve.

Lastly, the external roles of major Western states—primarily the U.S. but also the UK—are very important for the Baltic Sea area as well. If the U.S. continues its current policy of frequent military exercises in the Baltic Sea area—such as the Sabre Strike and Baltic Host series—this means an embedding of the U.S. military in the area, even if only at trip-wire force levels. In its turn, this provides necessary military weight in the area's local balance of power, given the very limited defense forces of the NB8 countries. A physical military withdrawal of the U.S. armed forces from the area—leaving the U.S. commitment at the rhetorical level—would be a disaster for the Baltic Sea area as a whole, since the balance of power of the whole region would then become utterly unstable.

In terms of other important actors, the UK has initiated a new format—the *Northern Group*, which includes the NB8, the UK and sometimes also Poland, Germany and the Netherlands—which has a clear-cut defense-related potential, and which squares very well with the concept of a Baltic Sea security complex. Keeping the UK interested in Baltic Sea security must also be considered as very healthy for the area.

Thus, to summarize the findings, it seems to be fair to say that the NB8 countries form a security complex, both among themselves and together with the rest of the Baltic Sea countries. The NB8 complex clearly has the potential to be transformed into a true security community, but this will demand strong political leadership in some of the countries involved—not least concerning the prospect of Sweden's and Finland's eventual NATO membership.

It is harder to predict whether the whole Baltic Sea area security complex will be transformed into a true security community. Such a community would require the eventual integration of Russia into Western Europe. However, this would among other things demand a profound change of Russian foreign policy toward the Baltic states and a transformation of Baltic-Russian relations. This seems today to be a tall order.

Chapter Seven

Embedding and Integration of the Nordic-Baltic Region: A U.S. Perspective

Daniel P. Fata

For anyone watching the Nordic-Baltic region during the past decade or so, developments in joint military cooperation, information sharing, capability development, and expeditionary deployment among and between the nations of Norway, Denmark, Sweden, Finland, Iceland, Lithuania, Latvia, and Estonia have been both significant and enviable. Accomplishments such as the establishment of joint defense colleges and joint officer exchanges, joint support to air policing missions, joint missions to Kosovo and Afghanistan, and the establishment of a Nordic Battle Group within the European Union are just a few of the milestones achieved by the Nordic or Baltic nations acting together, and, in some cases, a combination of Nordic and Baltic nations working together.

The process was originally started by the Nordic countries in the early 1990s and expanded to include the Baltic nations in the late 1990s as Lithuania, Latvia, and Estonia started their preparations for membership in the North Atlantic Treaty Organization (NATO). The intent of the process was to help deepen cooperation between the Nordic, Baltic, and then Nordic-Baltic nations, to create greater common approaches and develop common standards between the participating nations, to achieve greater economies of scale and efficiency in doing things jointly or commonly, and to develop a regional security

Daniel P. Fata is Vice-President at the Cohen Group in Washington, D.C. and a Transatlantic Fellow at the German Marshall Fund of the U.S. From September 2005 to September 2008, he served as the U.S. Deputy Assistant Secretary of Defense for Europe and NATO Policy.

capacity and capability among like-minded, geographically-contiguous Northern European which could not only help strengthen regional security but also provide enhanced capabilities to NATO and the EU.

Along the way, the United States expressed its support, in word and deed, for such efforts. The U.S. has provided rotations of squadrons to conduct air policing missions in the Baltics, has participated in defense-focused annual Nordic-Baltic senior official meetings, and has provided support to partnership capacity efforts, as well as deployment support, including logistics movements and air-to-air refueling, to all of the Nordic-Baltic nations. However, U.S. consistency and proactivity in embedding and integrating directly into the Nordic-Baltic region as a whole has not been as aggressive as some might have hoped.

Given a range of factors including the global financial crisis, the continued decline of European defense budgets with a somewhat commensurate decline in defense capabilities, the withdrawal of additional U.S. forces from Europe, and the pending drawdown of Allied forces in Afghanistan post-2014, the time to shore up, embed, and integrate U.S.-Nordic-Baltic defense efforts has never seemed so ripe. Now is the time to examine why embedding and integration has made a difference in terms of regional security capability development and why such efforts will matter even greater going forward? What has been done to date in terms of embedding and integrating? What more can be done? What are the challenges to be overcome? And, finally, what role should the U.S. play in this integration?

Why Does Embedding and Integrating Matter and Why Will It Matter Even More Going Forward?

Embedding and integrating are necessary components of any successful military and security partnership. Understanding a partner's threat assessments, intentions, plans, and capabilities are essential in maintaining stability and peace with one's neighbors and being able to muster needed military assets when a crisis occurs. Canada and the U.S. have been embedded in each other's military institutions for more than half a decade. The U.S. and the UK also have a long history of embedding officers in headquarters as well as within military units. France, Germany, and the Netherlands have also undertaken similar actions including standing up the EuroCorps. The net result of all this has been a stronger working relationship between these nations, development of joint standards, increased interoperability, and a strengthening of the political bonds between the countries. All of this has been achieved while the nations have been part of the greatest embedder and integrator in the history of military alliances, i.e., NATO. The actions of individual nations to further strengthen bilateral and, in a regional sense, multilateral ties have not been at NATO's expense.

However, NATO faces some daunting challenges in the coming years, which only reinforces the need for nations to take steps to integrate more fully among them as a way of enhancing NATO's overall capabilities in the most efficient way possible. It will come as no surprise to those who follow European security issues that the trend lines for Europe to have full-spectrum defense and response capabilities do not look promising, and, in some cases, look extremely worrisome during the next decade. It is no secret that defense spending across all NATO and EU member states has declined during the past decade. Recently-released NATO headquarters statistics reveal that European defense spending has dropped significantly during the past ten years, with the average annual percentage of GDP being spent on national defense less than 1.4 percent. In fact, it is quite conceivable that had the ISAF mission not been undertaken by NATO, the amount of money spent on defense would have been even lower.

With Europe at relative peace in the post-Cold War era and with America continuing to maintain a dominant edge in nearly all aspects of defense and security (even though it, too, will be cutting its defense budget by nearly $500 billion during the next decade), the arguments and justifications made by European parliamentarians and governments for strong defense spending levels and capability enhancements have become harder and harder to make. Coupled with a global economic recession, a less-than-popular military campaign in Iraq, and a longer-than-expected and harder-than-expected military campaign in Afghanistan, the ability of politicians and political leaders to muster the political will to call for and then allocate the sufficient amount of national treasure to maintain robust military forces post-2014 when NATO forces withdraw from Afghanistan will be immensely challenging. Domestic concerns for greater social welfare spending, unemployment assistance, and simply the isolationist calls for a retreat back to Fortress Europe or to the shores of the Atlantic and Pacific protecting America and Canada will only get louder in the next few years. In the United States, this can already be seen by the return of two of its four Army brigades stationed in Europe.

Doing whatever possible to avoid a catastrophic collapse of European military capabilities is necessary. Operations in Afghanistan and Libya have demonstrated that the allies have what it takes when called upon to conduct missions to support national, NATO, EU, and UN goals. However, these missions have also revealed that nations do not train the same way, develop capabilities the same way, nor do they have similar capacities with respect to logistics, intelligence and surveillance, munitions, rotary wing aircraft, air-to-air refueling, and night fighting capabilities, among others.

And while it is unrealistic to expect individual nation states to have full-spectrum defense capabilities to fight or operate in every conceivable environment and contingency, it is not ridiculous to accept the current argument and thinking that nations can be smarter about how they procure defense capabilities and how they use them in relation to other allies and partners. This is precisely the idea behind NATO Secretary General Rasmussen's proposed "smart defense" initiative of getting allies to think more carefully about what and how they procure defense items, how it integrates into their national inventory, how it relates to overall national, Alliance, and EU needs, and how these assets can be used as leverage with other partners' assets to actually increase overall capability in necessary areas while maximizing efficiency, avoiding redundancy as well as different standards, and ensuring such assets are available for wide use. There is an argument also to be made that developing expertise and niche capabilities such as mountain warfare fighting, counterinsurgency training, or anti-piracy enhance overall security for a region or an alliance even if all members are not participating in that training or endeavor.

The bottom line is that embedding and integration have been essential elements of defense planning within NATO and among its member states for decades. Such actions have enhanced security throughout the region. New initiatives should be encouraged and, given the experiences of the past decade in terms of deployments in Iraq, Afghanistan, and Libya, the transformation and modernization efforts which took place earlier in the 2000s, and the continuing economic challenges facing the entire Europe-Eurasia-North America region, the time to launch the "2.0" version of these initiatives is upon us. How those initiatives are developed, implemented, and shared will be crucial.

What More Can Be Done with Embedding and Integrating in the Nordic-Baltic Region?

One of the exciting components of the existing embedding and integration initiative launched by the Nordic and Baltic countries is the scalability inherent in its design. The Nordic nations have been very practical and pragmatic in creating a list of achievable tasks and projects in order to validate the concept that embedding and integrating soldiers and officers in each others' war colleges has benefits and works, that developing joint training standards makes sense, and that joint exercises, missions, and deployments—whether near or abroad— is executable. At one point, there was a list of nearly 100 individual tasks and projects the Nordic nations themselves desired to achieve in terms of further embedding and integrating—and most could be realistically achieved within a ten-year period assuming financial resources and political will continued to be constant factors.

The Baltic nations themselves achieved great success in the establishment of a Baltic Defense College, joint air policing support packages for NATO allies to help patrol Baltic air space, a joint Baltic radar center, and other Baltic-centric initiatives. These projects were heavily supported by Denmark and Norway and eventually other NATO nations, including the U.S. and the U.K., and have continued to grow in scale and complexity.

Now is the time to take the already laudable achievements by the Nordic and Baltic nations and deepen these projects both within the region itself as well as within specific task sets and also to broaden the projects to include more of northern Europe and NATO. The intent should be to not only shore up the work among these nations during the past decade but also to help ameliorate the pending further decline in European defense budgets and capabilities. There are three specific areas in which this deepening and broadening can take place:

- Afghanistan Lessons Learned
- Cyberdefense
- High North

Afghanistan. All eight Nordic-Baltic nations deployed some amount of military (and, in Iceland's case non-military) personnel to Afghanistan as part of the UN-sanctioned International Security Assistance Force (ISAF) mission. Norway, Sweden, and Finland continue to jointly reside and operate in northern Afghanistan, while Denmark, Latvia, and Estonia operate in southern Afghanistan, and Lithuania runs a Provincial Reconstruction Team in Chaghcharan, which is one of the most environmentally-challenging areas in all of Afghanistan. Along with NATO's Joint Forces Command in Brunssum, each of the nations have conducted their own lessons learned regarding their time on the ground in Afghanistan. A great deal has been learned about how to jointly conduct operations but equally important is what has been learned regarding how to jointly deploy and sustain forces and equipment on the ground in inhospitable places far away from traditional centers of logistical and supply support. All of these lessons learned should be shared and institutionalized within the region, but also with NATO and with organizations who get involved in peace support and peacekeeping operations such as the UN, OSCE, African Union. The lessons learned should also be shared with the EU as part of its 18-unit Battle Group structure. The Nordic Battle Group is an ideal formation and forum to build upon the achievements made in joint deployment and operations to ensure other Battle Groups as well as NATO Response Force (NRF) units also understand how joint logistics, rapid response teams, expeditionary medical treatment, and a range of other issues are addressed. In terms of laying out a path for enhancing further embedding and integration among Nordic-Baltic militaries with regard to operations, there is probably no better testbed and concept validator than the ISAF mission.

Cyber Center of Excellence. Nearly four years ago, Estonia established a Cooperative Cyber Defense Center of Excellence (COE) in

Tallinn. The COE was created following a cyber attack on Estonia allegedly originating from Russia. While COE's are not NATO-funded, they are accredited by NATO and allies and partners can either support or contribute to the COE's operations and programming. The threat of cyber attack continues to grow with potential aggressors emanating from states, non-state actors, and individuals, some with malicious intent, while others may test defenses just to see if they can crack the system. Regardless, Estonia is taking the lead in working on cyber defense issues which will be of great benefit to the Alliance, the EU, the U.S., and other partners around the world. A simple and relatively cost-effective means of strengthening Estonia's efforts would be for the Nordic-Baltic nations to jointly establish, sponsor, and fund a cyber defense cell within the COE focused on Nordic-Baltic cyber issues and efforts currently being undertaken nationally to address cybersecurity. While the internet is global and boundless in its reach, a cyberattack on any of the Nordic-Baltic regions could have serious economic, environmental, military, and legal ramifications for its neighbors with some potential disastrous spillover effects. Launching a concerted regional cybersecurity working group with a focused exercise plan matched with a robust lessons learned effort will not only be beneficial to the region, but will enhance the COE's legitimacy and value as a practical resource to be used by NATO and other countries within Europe and beyond.

High North "Action Group." Increasingly the world is being made aware of the climate changes affecting the Earth particularly in the Arctic where ice packs are continuing to melt and previously non-navigable sea lanes are starting to open, albeit for brief periods of time. In addition, the constant quest to find new sources of energy has led Russia and others to try and map the Arctic seabed and, in some cases, claim parts of undersea territory as an extension of national boundaries. And while there are only five Arctic littoral states (U.S., Canada, Russia, Norway, and Denmark) and eight members of the Arctic Council (U.S., Canada, Russia, Norway, Denmark, Iceland, Sweden, and Finland), all of Europe would be affected by a militarization of the Arctic region as well as by a race and competition for resources in the High North, as it is sometimes referred. Along with cyber defense, if there is an issue that would allow the Nordic-Baltic region to deepen its internal cooperation and provide value outside the region as well as not be seen solely as acting on a NATO or an EU-focused issue, it might well be the High North. And while establishing a High North COE may be a bridge too far at this time, it is conceivable that, in working with the Arctic Council, a center or "Action Group" could be established to work with the Council to develop areas for joint cooperation among littorals and Council members including the holding of joint annual exercises among littorals, non-littorals, and international organizations such as NATO, the EU, and the UN in maritime disaster response, air and sea rescue, and scientific exploration (including seabed mapping and oil, gas, and fisheries evaluations). An even more ambitious concept would be to have this Action Group develop a rapid response capability to assist with disaster response and rescue missions. Such an Action Group would directly involve the Nordic states but also provide opportunities for the Baltic countries as well as other European nations to jointly monitor and cooperate in ensuring the Arctic remains an area free from competition and possibly jointly develop doctrine and protocols for handling issues occurring in this difficult environment.

What Role Should the U.S. Play in Nordic-Baltic Regional Embedding and Integration?

It is often said that when the U.S. does not lead, nothing gets done. Another take on this is that when the U.S. does not participate, the action or mission or initiative will not succeed. And while an argument can be made that there is some validity to this (NATO Response Force, Strategic Airlift Consortium both became successful because of U.S. involvement and the NRF floundered when the U.S. decided to remove its contributions to annual rotations), NATO's recent Libya operation shows NATO can undertake missions where the U.S. is not in the lead (again, an argument can be made that the U.S. continued to play a linchpin role even though it was not "leading" the mission). Nordic, Baltic, and then Nordic-Baltic integration efforts have largely been undertaken by the respective nations themselves and supported by one other with U.S. "leadership." True, the U.S. did lend political support to these initiatives as well as financial support to the Baltic nations, but the integration projects were largely created by and implemented by the Nordic and Baltic nations.

During the past decade, the U.S. has contributed military and financial assets in support of joint U.S-Nordic-Baltic exercises and has provided partnership capacity training monies to support Baltic needs. With the reduction in U.S. forces in Europe to take place in the coming years and with U.S. forces beginning a drawdown in Afghanistan, the opportunity for Washington to shore up its commitment to northern Europe, let alone Europe writ large, needs to be done. Increasing U.S. military participation in joint Nordic-Baltic-U.S. exercises is an easy step to take and should be done. Lending financial support to Estonia's COE to support a Nordic-Baltic cybercell would also send a strong message. Perhaps other areas to consider would include providing excess defense articles, i.e. ground vehicles, helicopters and communication equipment that is being used presently in Afghanistan by U.S. forces which could then be used as training equipment for simulations and exercises among Nordic-Baltic-U.S. forces. Rotational training deployments of U.S. forces flowing to the Nordic-Baltic region could also be increased and made regular. Another possibility may be having mixed embedded crews on U.S. AEGIS cruisers which provide a mobile platform for U.S. and NATO missile defense efforts.

The important message Washington would send to northern Europe and beyond is that the U.S. supports and recognizes the integration efforts taking place in the Nordic-Baltic region, that such initiatives have improved bilateral and regional security arrangements, that the U.S. and NATO have benefitted from these projects, that creativity in terms of capability development and costs savings are being taken seriously by committed allies, and that the U.S. wants not only to foster further enhancements of these initiatives but to be part of them because it also enhances U.S. defense capabilities as well as tightens the bonds between America and its northern European allies. What the U.S. should not do is take any steps which reduce the entrepreneurialism that has existed among the Nordic-Baltic countries. It should, though, seek to increase its support to these initiatives and find a role to participate and build on the success already created.

Challenges to Future Embedding and Integration

The future of a deeper and wider embedding and integration process throughout the region is not guaranteed and will not organically develop without a dedicated core group of individuals willing to oversee and drive the process. As noted above, financial and budgetary issues will likely serve as the greatest governor or moderator of how ambitious any further steps will be concerning regional security integration in the near term. In addition to the overall distraction associated with the global financial crisis and how each nation deals itself with the consequences of it, other challenges will have an effect on the future of the integration endeavors. Those additional challenges include maintaining overall as well as individual national momentum, and political and military leaders' commitment throughout the Nordic-Baltic region. Ensuring adequate financial resources are available to fund existing projects and to launch second-phase projects will be a continuing challenge, as well as ensuring the capabilities developed are used regularly so that the benefits of embedding and integration are seen by not only those who mustered the political will to launch the initiatives but also by those who opposed the initiative arguing that such integration would not work.

For the initiative to truly be seen as successful, and this in some ways is the initiative's biggest challenge, is to demonstrate that the elements of this Nordic-Baltic embedding and integration process can be applied to regional security, NATO, EU, and global security issues. In addition, these elements need to be measured in terms of scale and effectiveness, the elements have the ability to be improved, and, finally, that the elements are able to be shared with other nations, other organizations within Europe, across the Atlantic, and around the world. Validation, application, and replication will be three key components when determining whether the Nordic-Baltic initiative has been successful and can be a model for other regional security projects.

Section III

Russia and the East

Chapter Eight

Putin Redux:
Foreign Policy under
Russia's Comeback President

Jana Kobzová and Tomáš Valášek

On May 7th 2012, Vladimir Putin will resume the presidency in Russia. His return will be a closely-watched affair: how, if at all, will Russia be different from that of the Medvedev era? In foreign policy terms, most of the commentary suggests that change, if any, will be minimal. Putin has never *not* been in charge; all the main decisions—such as the war in Georgia, the New START agreement with the U.S.—needed his approval, if not his actual hand in design. A more nuanced version of this argument holds that while Putin has at least tolerated all key foreign policy decisions, Dmitry Medvedev has been different from him. And importantly, because he does not hold the incoming president's fears and suspicions of the West, he sought compromises in disputes, from which Putin would have walked away in anger.[1]

The authors of this article went to Russia recently to speak to diplomats, analysts, journalists and other observers of Russian foreign policy. This paper argues that on balance, the latter of the two aforementioned views of Russian foreign policy seems more accurate: while Medvedev has never held much power, his relatively modern views on global affairs were felt in some key policies, such as the U.S.-Russian "reset." Unlike Putin, who as president antagonized Washington and played divide and rule with the Europeans, Medvedev saw cooperation with the United States and Europe as one of the steps towards Russia's

---

The authors are, respectively, policy fellow at the European Council on Foreign Relations and director of foreign policy and defence at the Centre for European Reform.

[1] See for example Charles Grant, "Will Putin Delete the Reset?" *New York Times*, April 4, 2012.

modernization, rather than as a sign of weakness. Correspondingly, the odds are that Russian foreign policy without him in the presidency will be less friendly to the West. U.S.-Russian ties will suffer the most from Putin's return. Russia's relations with its neighbors, however, will be less affected by the change in the Kremlin than by events in the neighborhood itself. There is little daylight on the subject between the outgoing and the incoming presidents; most key actors in Moscow agree that Russia should try to maximize its influence in, and control over, the former Soviet republics, though the definition of 'control' has changed in recent years. If Ukraine, Belarus and other neighbors continue to give Moscow the openings to consolidate power in the 'near abroad', Putin will take them, just as Medvedev would have.

In domestic political terms, the opposition's influence on the government will be stronger than at any time in recent years; politics has truly 'returned' to Russia, along with a consequential and competitive discourse on some policy matters such as economics. But foreign policy is not among them: the opposition has had very little to say on the subject and on certain issues, such as relations with the U.S., it is completely divided (not surprising for a coalition that includes liberals as well as hardline nationalists). When it comes to Russia's immediate neighborhood, even the 'liberals' tend to be quite hawkish. So a somewhat more democratic Russia will not necessarily become a friendlier power to its neighbors.

Russia's Foreign Policy: Key Principles

Since the collapse of the Soviet Union, two key ambitions have driven Russia's foreign policy. At the global level, Moscow sought to preserve its influence through permanent membership on the UN Security Council, its huge nuclear arsenal and its (relatively) large economy; at the regional level, the goal is to assert Russia's dominant position in the post-Soviet region (with the exception of the Baltic countries) and become a power on a par with key European states such as Germany. While these ambitions have remained more or less constant over the past two decades, Russia has adjusted the way in which it pursues its goals.

Throughout the 1990s and early 2000s, Moscow devoted much of its foreign policy energy and funds to transforming its former Soviet empire into a sphere of influence. By providing cheap energy resources, maintaining low tariffs, and holding its doors open to migrants from most of the twelve post-Soviet states, Moscow kept the region economically integrated with Russia. It has also sponsored a number of political re-integration projects including the Common-wealth of Independent States (CIS) and smaller, sector-focused group-ings such as the Collective Security Treaty Organization or Single Economic Space. Moreover, Russia retained military bases across the region and intervened in a number of conflicts, sometimes sending forces against the host-countries' will. This combination of policies allowed Moscow to remain a regional hegemon for most of the 1990s and early 2000s.

Perhaps paradoxically, as Russia grew richer, it also became more reluctant to subsidize its post-Soviet allies. During Putin's first two terms in office, Moscow started to demand concrete concessions from its allies, such as the control of their strategic assets or the extension of Russia's military presence on their territories, if they wanted to benefit from cheap energy or preferential access to the Russian market. When countries such as Georgia or Ukraine ventured outside Moscow's orbit and chose to pursue EU and NATO membership, Russia responded with political and economic pressure including trade embargoes and gas cut-offs.

Yet for all its integration efforts, Moscow has found its ambitions for the post-Soviet space constrained by its neighbors' unwillingness to become Russian satellites, as well as the presence of other actors such as the EU or China in the region. In Eastern Europe and the south Caucasus, Brussels offered its own quasi-integrationist project to the former Soviet republics and currently promotes the political and economic association of the region with the EU via its 'Eastern Partnership'. The EU's impact on democracy in these countries has been limited at best. However, its increasing economic presence and political co-operation has allowed these states to diversify their economies and foreign policies away from over-dependence on Russia. In Central Asia, China's increased interest in the region's energy resources similarly limited Russia's influence. Central Asia now pro-vides ten percent of China's gas and oil needs; it has become an important element in Beijing's energy security strategy[2]. Beijing has also broken Russia's monopoly on the transit of hydrocarbons in the region by joining forces with central Asian states to build China-bound gas and oil pipelines. China has also become more active in addressing security threats in the region, and is driving co-operation on these issues in the framework of the Shanghai Cooperation Organization (SCO), much to Russia's discomfort. "The SCO has turned into a Chinese-dominated body," the authors were recently told in Moscow.

These changes do not imply that Russia has lost all of its influence in the region to Europe or China—the EU itself is struggling to turn its increasing economic presence in Eastern Europe into meaningful political leverage, and the Central Asians are wary of growing Chinese influence. But the EU's and Beijing's presence in the region means that Russia's own integration ambitions for the post-Soviet space have had to be re-thought. Russian officials now acknowledge that a full re-integration of the post-Soviet space "is impossible,"[3] while previous attempts to pursue it through energy and other subsidies became a drain on the Russian treasury.

Rethinking CIS policy under Medvedev

Under Medvedev's presidency, Russia radically reconsidered its approach to the post-Soviet space. Although the start of his presidential term was marked by Russia's war with Georgia, fears of a similarly assertive attitude towards Russia's other neighbors have gradually subsided. In hindsight, what many considered the prelude to Russia's renewed expansionism proved to be its climax.

There remains a broad consensus among the Russian elite that Moscow should maintain a dominant influence in the post-Soviet space. It was the liberal think-tank INSOR, whose chairman is no other than Medvedev himself, which argued in one of its studies that the Collective Security Treaty Organization (CSTO) should have the

---

[2] "China Analysis: The new Great Game in Central Asia," European Council on Foreign Relations and Asia Centre, September 6, 2011.

[3] Remarks by Grigory Karasin, Deputy Secretary of the Russian Ministry of Foreign Affairs, at the International Institute for Security Studies, London, July 1, 2011.

right to intervene on their members' territory without the consent of all CSTO states[4]. But this widespread consensus is becoming increasingly incompatible with Russia's economic means. During Medvedev's presidency, in 2008–2009, Russia experienced the worst economic downturn among the G20 countries. Since then, it has grown reluctant to bear the full political and economic costs of restoring the post-Soviet space into a union. Instead of full reintegration, Moscow is now deploying its limited resources more selectively across the region, focusing on a few strategic priorities, such as gaining control over energy infrastructure and other key economic assets, or retaining military bases (all of which also open avenues for Russia's political influence in the region). Moscow also spends more time and attention on some countries than on others, with Belarus, Kazakhstan, and Ukraine at the top of the list. This new approach allows Moscow to conserve resources while remaining the ultimate political arbiter in these countries. In effect, under Medvedev, the Kremlin launched a new strategy tailored for a more limited sphere of influence—one that the ECFR described as a "lily-pad empire."[5]

In practice, the revamped neighborhood has meant that when promoting economic integration in the post-Soviet space through the Customs Union and Common Economic Space, Moscow has dealt primarily with Ukraine, Belarus and Kazakhstan. Whereas previously, similar projects were aimed at all CIS countries, this time Moscow focused solely on the countries where economic integration can bring the greatest economic gains for Russia itself (when Kyrgyzstan expressed interest in joining the Customs Union, Russia remained lukewarm). This new streamlined approach is no smaller challenge for the West than Moscow's all-encompassing attitude was previously: a 'lily-pad' strategy consumes fewer Russian resources while allowing Moscow to build up levers of influence over key local partners; these

---

[4] Vladimir Socor, "Medvedev-led think tank proposes reinforcing Russia-led CSTO," *Eurasia Daily Monitor*, volume 8, issue 164, September 8, 2011.

[5] See Ben Judah, Jana Kobzova and Nicu Popescu, "Dealing with a post-BRIC Russia," European Council on Foreign Relations, November 2011. The term "lily-pad empire" is borrowed from Donald Rumsfeld, who proposed that the US military should abandon its large, quasi-permanent bases in favor of smaller "lily-pad" deployments in strategic locations.

levers in turn can be deployed to keep them from distancing themselves from Russia in the future.

The efforts to promote closer integration with the trio of Kazakhstan, Belarus, and Ukraine are likely to continue during Putin's next presidential term as well. However, both Ukraine and Belarus are almost perfect examples of the limits of Russian power; events across the Russian borders, rather than personnel in the Kremlin, have shaped, and will continue to shape, Russia's relations with neighbors.

Forward to the Past:
What Putin's Return Means for Russia's Foreign Policy

While events in Eastern Europe will have more effect on Russia's neighborhood policy than the leadership swap in the Kremlin, a few possible changes could follow Putin's inauguration in May. Our conversations in Moscow suggest that re-integration of the former Soviet republics in general—and of Ukraine in particular—remains high on Moscow's foreign policy agenda, as it has been for a number of years, even if Russia's strategies for the neighborhood have evolved. The 'near abroad' seems likely to receive somewhat more attention under Vladimir Putin: the president-elect's first in a series of pre-election articles on Russia's future was devoted entirely to the need to build a 'Eurasian Union', a sort of EU for the East, under Russian leadership.[6] "As prime minister, Putin focused on the post-Soviet space, leaving relations with the U.S. and EU to Medvedev," one observer said. This fits in with the two men's worldviews; while the pursuit of a partnership with the EU and U.S. has been, to Russia, a modernizing endeavor, reintegration as proposed by Putin is a project from the past. It is about recreating something that Russia views as its own, which had been 'lost'—a core Putin belief.

At the same time, as with many other foreign policy issues, the Eurasian Union is getting far less attention than its successful implementation would require. For example, Putin's article specifically mentions the EU as a model but there is little sign of Russia studying the costs and benefits that EU member-states incurred when integrating,

---

[6] Vladimir Putin, "New Integration Project for Eurasia—A Future That Is Being Born Today," *Izvestiya*, October 4, 2011.

Case Study I: Ukraine's Stealth Loss of Sovereignty

It was under the influence of the 'modernizing' Dmitry Medvedev that Ukraine lost more sovereignty to Moscow than at any period during Vladimir Putin's reign. Going by present trends, the country seems certain to come under an even stronger Russian spell in the future—though not because of Vladimir Putin's return.

The reasons lie almost entirely in Kyiv itself. Viktor Yanukovich has handled Russia's desire for greater control over Ukraine particularly badly. For decades, Kyiv's strategy has been relatively simple: while some governments were more openly friendly to Moscow than others, all stuck to two principles: keep Russian investors from acquiring sensitive assets such as gas infrastructure (and thus reduce Moscow's ability to use economic levers to political ends), and pursue close relations with the West so as to have powerful friends to balance Moscow. Yanukovich broke the latter rule, and may soon be forced to break the former one too.

The President's single-minded emphasis on consolidating domestic control has effectively sabotaged relations with the US and the European Union. His persecution of former Prime Minister Yulia Tymoshenko bears marks of a selective application of justice and the EU is increasingly concerned about the fairness of Ukraine's upcoming parliamentary elections. The US has criticized the government for hounding journalists seen as unfriendly to the regime. Ukraine's prospect of EU membership has receded, as its friendship with Washington has suffered, and with it, so has Kyiv's ability to balance Moscow.

Russia has seized the opening. It is pressing Ukraine to join the Customs Union, hinting at a possible boycott of its goods should it fail to do so. Moscow has extended Kyiv no courtesy of reducing gas prices, as it did to Germany and a few other European customers; Ukraine continues to pay crippling rates. Kyiv may soon be forced to sell parts of Naftogaz, its energy giant, to Russia, in order to avoid default on its gas bill. If Naftogaz is sold, Ukraine's ability to reform its inefficient energy sector and reduce dependency on Russian gas—the country's greatest vulnerability—will be seriously weakened.

Viktor Yanukovich probably never intended this—he maintains that EU integration is Ukraine's top foreign policy priority. But he and his ministers appear to have misread the EU: they are wrongly assuming that Ukraine would be welcome because of its size and location, and that it would not be held to the same rules and values as other countries vying for membership in, or at least privileged relations with, the EU. In practice, Yanukovich's steps have not only alienated the West but have also made it very difficult for his successors to reverse Ukraine's foreign policy course. One Ukrainian entrepreneur told the author in 2010: "The real worry is not that Yanukovich will hand over Ukraine to Russia by design; it is that he will do so through sheer incompetence." If present trends continue, that businessperson may be proven right.

If it happens, it would represent less Russia's success than Ukraine's failure. Consecutive Moscow governments, under both Putin and Medvedev, have sought to keep Ukraine from leaving Russia's side: most Russians think of it as an "independent country, but not a foreign one," as one observer in Moscow pointed out. The only difference between Putin's and Medvedev's reigns has been that Kyiv presented the latter leader many more opportunities to reinforce Russian influence than it ever did under Putin. But both men have been keen to keep Ukraine close, and Putin, heavily assisted by Viktor Yanukovich, seems well positioned to finish the job of reintegration that has seen so much progress under Medvedev.

Case Study II: Belarus' Botched Balancing Act

In political terms, Belarus has long been more tightly integrated with Russia than any other former Soviet state. But it was during Medvedev's presidency that Russia managed to substantially expand its economic footprint as well, while adding to its political clout, in Belarus.

Minsk has participated in every integration blueprint that Moscow produced for the post-Soviet space. Yet much of it remained on paper only: while Belarusian president Aliaksandr Lukashenka kept good ties with Moscow, he was careful not to allow Russian state companies to penetrate the Belarusian economy to such a point, which would limit his own freedom for maneuver. To this end, Lukashenka reached out to the European Union every time Russia's pressure on Minsk increased; he has been performing a careful balancing act between Brussels and Moscow.

But since early 2011, the Belarusian president has found himself isolated from the EU and at the mercy of Russia like never before. Following the rigged presidential elections in December 2010 and the subsequent crackdown on civil society, the EU has imposed visa bans and frozen assets of more than 230 individuals including Lukashenka and his closest circle of financiers. For Minsk, the freezing of the relations came at the worst possible time: thanks to a pre-election spending spree, the regime was in dire need of a cash injection. The EU and U.S. signaled that Belarus would receive no stabilization loan from the IMF unless it released all political prisoners. Lukashenka refused, and instead sought economic help from Russia. Moscow responded positively: it arranged a $3 billion loan from the Eurasian Economic Community, provided a $1 billion loan to Belarus' potash-maker Belaruskali and gave Minsk a gas discount amounting to $2.5-3 billion per year. However, this economic cushion was conditioned by Belarus launching a new privatization program, which Russia envisaged would be conducive to its own economic interests. Moscow's strategy has paid off: in November 2011, Gazprom gained full ownership of Belarus' gas transit operator Beltransgas, despite Minsk's previous adamant refusals to sell the company to Russian ownership. To prompt Lukashenka to open up even more privatization opportunities to Moscow, Russia has recently started to reduce the flow of crude oil to the Druzhba pipeline, which crosses Belarus, and instead it ships more crude to Europe via the BTS2 terminal in Saint Petersburg, thus depriving Belarus of lucrative revenue. In recent weeks, Moscow also threatened to stop importing Belarusian milk, and the two countries came close to interrupting all air travel following the latest dispute over the frequency of flights between them.[7]

Unless Minsk quickly mends its relations with the EU, the incoming president Putin may well be presented with possibilities of influence in Belarus that Russia had never enjoyed before. If the selling-out of the Belarusian economy to Russia continues, the country may lose more sovereignty than any other state in Eastern Europe.

or their reasons and strategies for doing so. The Eurasian Union, like those integration projects before, may end up half-finished. But even a partial union would have benefits for Moscow: a tighter economic integration of Ukraine, for example, would allow important sectors of Russian industry such as steel and fertilizer producers to effectively eliminate competition from Ukraine (because without barriers to investment, Russian businesses would most probably buy their Ukrainian counterparts). Ownership of Belarus' energy transit infrastructure has already eliminated the role of Minsk as a potentially stubborn intermediary in transit of Russia's EU-bound energy supplies.

The one new element shaping Russian foreign policy under Putin will be the domestic political debate. One of the objectives of the current leadership in Moscow is to protect the internal political system from outside interference. While the opposition has failed to prevent Putin's return, it remains on the scene as an active force, more willing to challenge the government than at any time in recent memory. Its success in attracting a hundred thousand people to anti-Putin demonstrations underscores that the incoming president has lost some of his popularity. This could be important for Moscow's future foreign policy: if Putin's regime suffers another crisis of legitimacy—and if the opposition is seen as capitalizing on the crisis—the Kremlin may try to boost its support by stirring up trouble abroad, much as Putin did

---

[7] For more on Russia's latest economic pressure on Belarus, see Siarhei Bohdan, "Trade Wars With Russia: From Sugar To Airlines," *BelarusDigest*, April 2, 2012.

during the presidential elections (when he accused Washington of being the 'puppet master' behind the popular protests).

However, if and when Putin needs to divert attention from domestic woes, he is more likely to pick on the United States than neighbors or the EU. Conversations with people familiar with his thinking suggest that the incoming president genuinely views Washington as a threat to his regime. Tellingly, when Putin's personal popularity reached its lowest point early this year, he stopped talking of the Eurasian Union and honed in on the U.S.

Recommendations for the EU and the U.S.

The goals for the U.S. and the EU in Eastern Europe are simple: to help the states maintain their right of self-determination, to assist their economic development, and to safeguard and expand political freedoms in the region. In theory, these goals do not clash with Russia's vision for Eastern Europe; even Vladimir Putin's article on the Eurasian Union stressed that states would join it voluntarily. And Russia and the West do share important interests in stemming the drug trade and terrorist activities in Central Asia. But the existing limited co-operation obscures a deeper underlying disagreement. In practice, the two sides offer very different societal models to Eastern Europe. One emphasizes individual freedoms more than the other; in one, governments play a limited and often reluctant role in the economy, whereas in the other, the government is often a tool for capturing economic benefits.

Russia's foreign policy will make it more difficult for the EU and the U.S. to advance their societal model in Eastern Europe—indeed, at times this seems like the express purpose of Russian foreign policy. The response of the EU and the United States will inevitably be affected by the economic crisis and the broader crisis of confidence. These aspects have made the West less attractive to the East; they have also hamstrung the EU because so many member-states' governments have turned against further enlargement. The EU can no longer credibly use membership as an incentive to prompt countries to liberalize and modernize. But even with this somewhat limited toolset, the West has several effective policies at its disposal:

- *Make energy reforms a priority in Eastern Europe.* Gas and oil dependence on Russia are among the countries' greatest vulnerabilities; lack of transparency in the energy sector has also corrupted an entire generation of politicians in Ukraine and elsewhere. Kyiv and Chisinau have joined the European 'energy community', and thus have agreed to implement the EU's laws on the subject, including the obligation to legally separate ownership of pipelines from ownership of their content. If implemented, such 'unbundling' holds the promise of breaking energy monopolies such as Naftogaz in Ukraine. The EU should hold Ukraine and Moldova to their obligations, and remain ready to support their energy reforms with money and expertise.

- *Intervene quickly when democracy is being subverted.* In Ukraine, the EU eventually began speaking out clearly against Viktor Yanukovich's violations of freedoms of speech and his treatment of Yulia Tymoshenko; it now (rightly) refuses to ratify an association agreement with Kyiv until freedoms in Ukraine improve. But the EU missed opportunities to nip these undemocratic tendencies in the bud. Yanukovich set about amassing power very early in his presidency; within a few months of his inauguration in 2010 the intimidation of journalists and harassment of the opposition began. Yet it took nearly another year for the EU to respond loudly and clearly (the U.S. Secretary of State Hillary Clinton did so long before the EU). By initially muting their criticism, the EU gave Yanukovich reasons to think that Ukraine would be able to integrate with the EU while limiting freedoms at home—Europe thus lost the ability to use Ukraine's desire for EU membership to curb Yanukovich's undemocratic tendencies.

- *Engage in Belarus' transformation, not isolation.* While the current troubles are entirely of Lukashenka's own making, a weak and isolated Belarus is easy prey for Moscow. The EU should reconsider its current policy of sanctions and instead focus on increasing interaction with ordinary Belarusians, expanding business and human links with the country. While restarting the suspended projects inside Belarus, the EU should keep those responsible for the fate of political prisoners on its visa ban list for as long as they remain in prison. Such policy will be consistent both with EU's values as well as its ambition to promote greater interaction with its neighbors.

This, admittedly, is a somewhat modest set of recommendations—hardly 'game changing' in nature. The reality of Western policy towards the Eastern neighborhood today is that the attention of the EU in particular has been almost entirely consumed by the economic crisis. The East is often seen as a distraction or, worse, as a source of cheap, illegal labor that undermines living standards in the West. Given these handicaps, the EU is poorly placed to lead, inspire and reform the neighborhood. But this is not to say that it should do nothing, and the above recommendations give the U.S. and EU countries a roadmap to make limited progress.

As for Russia itself, a conversation about common interests in the shared neighborhood needs to be a part of the Russo-Western dialogue. Similarly, the EU and the U.S. on the one hand, and Russia on the other, should use opportunities for pragmatic co-operation on issues such as the security of Afghanistan after NATO's withdrawal in 2012. However, these will not fundamentally change Russia's view of the neighborhood as an area where it desires to maintain dominant influence, and where it sees the West as a direct competitor. This has been the case under Medvedev, and will continue to be the case under Putin.

Chapter Nine

Eternal Russia and the Troublesome East

Urban Ahlin

After the recent presidential election in Russia, a feeling of resigna-
tion spreads. Those who believed in Medvedev as the liberal reformer
in Russian politics were horribly deceived. When Putin announced
that the two had long agreed that he would return as president, it was
a scornful smile to those who thought that Medvedev actually had had
his own agenda. Many were the diplomats who energetically stressed
the need to trust and support Medvedev. Some believed he was the
right man for Russia, others hoped to give him the necessary strength
to challenge Putin. Now we know that the presidential election had
been a fixed game for some time.

The methods used by Putin to win the election make me uncom-
fortable. I am not thinking primarily of electoral fraud or of the so-
called 'administrative' resources that were used. I think he would have
won the election even without electoral fraud and the help of administrative resources. What worries me is that Putin, during the election
campaign, again and again insisted that the election was decisive for
Russia's independence. What he actually told his voters was that foreign (Western) forces wanted to hurt Russia economically and politically, forcing it into submission.

What drives a president, who still has strong support despite the
demonstrations that took place mainly after the parliamentary elections, to use such doomsday rhetoric? Is it because Russian society is
full of anti-Western sentiments that Putin needed to draw on to win
the election? Or does Putin actually believe that Russia's independence is threatened by foreign forces? Either way, it shows we have a

Urban Ahlin is the Foreign Policy Spokesperson for the Social Democratic Party of
Sweden and Deputy Chair of the Foreign Relations Committee of the Parliament of
Sweden.

bumpy road ahead in our relations with Russia. Furthermore, it is proof that there is not much hope for a quick turnaround in Russian policy.

Someone once told me that elections in Russia are a battle between the TV Party and the Internet Party. The former being people who still only find their news via television, and the latter being those who increasingly find news on the Internet. There is no question that Putin has strong support among TV viewers and it is similarly certain that the support he has from Internet-users is significantly lower. Even though Internet users are increasing in number, I doubt that it will undermine Putin's power any time soon.

Is it finally time to give up on Russia and/or Putin? How should the world act now that it is clear that Putin will be in power for likely another 12 years? My own reflection is that not much has really happened. Putin's return as president is not a big deal because he never really left power in the first place. Medvedev never had the mandate for change that diplomats and other experts had hoped for. So why jump to conclusions when everything remains as it was before the election?

We should now closely observe if Putin II is different from Putin I. I would not bet much money that Putin II will pursue different policies from Putin I. But I do think that the EU and U.S. should give him the benefit of the doubt and see what he actually does in his second term of office. Political leaders have shown throughout history that they do not always repeat the same mistakes. They can change. Larger miracles have occurred.

The challenges Putin II faces are enormous. Russia's systemic corruption is the biggest of these challenges because it destroys competiveness in Russia and makes all investments extremely expensive. But is Putin really interested in combating the corruption, or does his powerbase depend on such kickbacks? If Putin II continues on the same path as before, where journalistic freedom is suppressed and journalists are killed; where corruption is allowed to flourish; and where the security apparatus increasingly is taking over businesses, it is absolutely necessary that the world reacts.

What Can One Do to Really Influence Russia?

Not much, is the sad but honest answer. It is important to remember that Russia of today is not the old Soviet Union. The Russian voters are increasingly demanding that their politicians deliver and take responsibility. There are positive signs in Russia but it is in spite of, rather than thanks to, the Russian political leaders.

Remember also that Russia is suffering from Post Imperialistic Stress. And this stress might take Russia decades, or even centuries, to recover from as was the case with former European colonial powers. Russian politicians often say that Russia must take back its rightful place in the world. But exactly what or where this rightful place is remains unanswered. The bottom line is that Russia wants to be respected and/or feared as it once was. Maybe one should see the Foreign Minister Lavrov's spoiling attempts in international affairs in this light. He ensures for Russian foreign policy a few minutes in the spotlight to give the Russian people a sense that their country is still respected or perhaps even feared. We all know though that they back down a couple of weeks later after the spotlight has moved away.

The sad thing is that the EU has too often fallen into the trap of being stressed by the Russians at EU-Russia summits, when nothing is delivered. Russia always wants summits to end in nice declarations and the EU always plays along, delivering declarations and promises of working groups here and there. Too many promises and excessive demands on performance at various summits have led to Russia benefiting from new concessions from the EU without living up to what they had earlier pledged. The relationship between the EU and Russia should be based more on common values and less on common interests. The EU must make clear to the Russians that the relationship demands that both parties stick to the agreements.

For me, the only way to influence Russia is to do so indirectly. Neighboring countries such as Ukraine, Georgia, and Belarus all lack the experience of market economy and democracy. So does Russia. If the neighboring countries could succeed with reform efforts it would have an impact on Russia. No one should underestimate the importance of Ukraine getting their politics and economics in order as a catalyst for Russia.

But for now, there are unfortunately few successes to report in the neighboring area. The color of the revolutions has faded. As today one can argue that only Moldova and Georgia have achieved any sort of success, while Belarus and Ukraine are unfortunately sliding back to the old ways.

Why Are These Eastern Countries So Troublesome?

The lack of experience with a market economy and democracy plays a vital role of course. An ingrained attitude that says that citizens are for the state and not the other way around is also creating obstacles. Above all though, I believe that a lack of positive incentives is the most important factor.

The Central European countries did have experience of democracy and of market economy but they also were determined to enter the two institutions of NATO and the EU. The doors to these institutions were open and so attractive to enter that the willingness to make reforms, many of which were painful, was very strong. Yes, there was an internal debate in NATO and the EU as to whether they should be admitted, and sometimes the debate was heated. However, most Central European countries realized early on that it would be seen as a historical failure not to make Europe whole and free.

NATO was a stepping stone on the long road to EU membership. It was easier to become a member of NATO than fulfilling all of the requirements in the EU aquis. And by using this stepping stone, politicians of all colors could show voters that their country was on its way to becoming an ordinary European state.

But how can this effort to reform come to fruition if the EU does not give countries even long-term membership prospects because of enlargement fatigue among EU countries? NATO cannot be used as a stepping stone as it was in the case of the Central European countries because the populations of Eastern Europe are heavily against membership of NATO in all countries but Georgia.

It is not a surprise that these Eastern countries seemingly never get out of the starting blocks. They lack experience with a market economy and democracy, their populations are opposed to NATO membership, and EU membership is considered unreachable, with the door closed due to enlargement fatigue among EU countries. So how can developments be influenced and necessary reforms promoted in these countries so that they, in future, will also affect Russia?

The best game in town is the EU's Eastern Partnership. The Eastern Partnership was initiated by Sweden and Poland as an idea to reach out to neighboring countries. The partnership promises close and deep cooperation and integration with the EU but stops short of promising future membership of the Union. The Eastern Partnership has so far contributed to the reform efforts in some countries but not all. Belarus is a notable exception as its relationship with the EU plummets. But Georgia, as well as Moldova and Armenia, have performed so well that the EU has promised to all three that negotiations will start on a DCFTA (Deep and Comprehensive Free Trade Area).

Some Eastern countries are using the Eastern Partnership in a fruitful way but others have not woken up to its potential benefits. One good thing from the Eastern Partnership that should not be overlooked is the fact that it has contributed to a lot more attention being given to this region from the EU than otherwise would have been the case.

How Can the Eastern Partnership Develop Further and Can the U.S. Play a Role?

To begin with, it is important to emphasize the conditionality of cooperation. Everything should be based on "more for more", but not to forget also "less for less". The U.S. should use the same method in its cooperation with the Eastern Partnership countries. The EU is now retooling its instruments of cooperation with both its eastern and southern neighborhoods. Of upmost importance is that the EU stops using geography as a factor in spending money. Today there is a de facto split of resources between southern neighbors that receive two thirds of the funding and the eastern neighbors that receive only one third. "More for more" as a method must be implemented. The EU must also dare to say "less for less" when the reforms do not occur and thus reduce support when countries do not deliver. The new European Neighborhood Instrument must be focused on the political objectives of the partnership and take into consideration the high costs of implementing the EU aquis in the Eastern Partnership countries.

The Eastern Partnership must build upon the amounts of various cooperative projects already initiated and should go further with an array of youth exchanges, cultural projects, scholarships for students, twinning programs, support for small and medium sized businesses, exchange of best practices, visa facilities, anti-corruption efforts, and strong support to civil societies. In all this work, transatlantic coordination and support from the U.S. could be of importance. After reaching the DCFTA the countries should be given help in preparing themselves for future entry to the internal market of the EU. A lot of support will be needed to help partner countries evaluate the laws and systems to see what has to be changed in order to enable participation in the internal market.

Attention should be focused on the lives of ordinary people. After all, they will ultimately decide in what direction their countries will go. When I first visited Belarus in the middle of the 1990s I met with university students who traveled regularly to Warsaw. The only cost they had to pay was a border crossing fee at approximately half a dollar and a train ticket. The students I met felt like Central Europeans. It was no problem at all to travel and to see and buy things, just as other Europeans did. Poland has since entered the Schengen area and students now have to get a visa and, even though many get visas for free, all too many Belarusians have to pay around 60 Euros. 60 Euros is a lot for ordinary people in Belarus. We in the West sometimes say that the Belarusian president Lukashenka is locking in his people and certainly he is now even preventing opposition leaders from leaving the country. But we should also acknowledge our own flaws. For many Belarusians we are locking them out from the EU. The visa costs must be removed or at least lowered to a minimum.

The need for financial assistance from the EU should be decided after a careful look at the countries' own resources. For instance, if a country is an exporter of oil and gas, then the support from the EU could be lowered significantly. Countries that do not have their own resources should get more support from the EU based on their achievements. One just needs to look at the different situation for

Azerbaijan and Armenia to understand that a model of one-size-fits-all is not appropriate.

The European Security Strategy rightly points out the need for secure and stable neighbors around Europe. Therefore it would be a good idea to bring the partner countries into the framework of CSDP (Common Security and Defense Policy). To have partner countries in crisis management operations should foster dialogue between militaries and civilians and lead to necessary security sector reforms. Training and educational programs like the Erasmus for militaries and diplomats in EU institutions should be open for partner countries as well. I personally question the need for battle groups in the EU. The costs of standing battle groups are huge and they lock in valuable resources for a long time. But as long as these remain, it might be a good idea to invite partner countries into the battle groups to give impetus for military reforms and also to build confidence between militaries.

On a final note, if the European Union does not manage to come out of its financial turmoil and get back on track promoting economic growth, then all of the above is useless. The EU will only promote positive changes in its neighborhood if the EU itself is an attractive power. Therefore maybe the best thing we can do for our neighbors at this point is to get our own house in order.

Chapter Ten

How to Handle Russia?
Some Practical Advice for the Nordic-Baltic
Countries and the U.S.

Kadri Liik

Ever since September 24, 2010, when Vladimir Putin announced his intention to return to the Kremlin, people in Western capitals have been looking for clues as to what his third term's foreign policy is likely to entail. In foreign policy, style matters. Dmitri Medvedev's smoother manner has made Russia an easier partner or neighbor for many, even though his willingness to engage in substantial coopera-tion with the West remained limited. His perceived zeal for domestic modernization never amounted to anything more than hype, and to that extent his real power remained a mystery to most, probably including Medvedev himself. Still, his term in the Kremlin offered a welcome respite from previous years' fruitless antagonism. The fear that Putin might bring back the thorny aggressive rhetoric of his sec-ond term is therefore understandable.

However, regardless of the course for which he opts, it will not be Putin's foreign policy that will inevitably compel the Western commu-nity to look for a new approach towards Russia, but rather the changed nature of his presidency. After 12 years, Russian society has overcome its political apathy. Putin has lost his semi-sacred status of 'national leader' and now faces discontent among the population and the elite at many levels, not only among urban professionals in large cities. The extent of this discontent varies as do the ways in which it is manifested but it will not disappear. Putin's ability to understand the nature of the new situation and to adapt to it remains questionable—and that in turn raises doubts about the sustainability of the regime.

Kadri Liik is a senior researcher at the International Centre for Defence Studies in Tallinn.

It seems to be clear in Washington, as well as in Berlin, that the major qualitative transformation that Russia is going through requires a new Western policy—one that would reach out to civil society and would prepare for possible changes, while at the same time maintaining a working relationship with the powers that be. Furthermore, even though Moscow's visibility on the international agenda has decreased and politicians have other more urgent policy problems on their minds, in some ways conditions have not been this conducive for a serious and sober debate on Russia for a long time. In the spring of 2012, the West's sentiments towards Russia are relatively unaffected by distorting factors, such as wishful thinking, excessive fears, strong personal relations between leaders or selfish bilateral agendas. In addition, the EU and NATO member countries are increasingly unanimous in their analyses of Russia. If, at the same time, their policy prescriptions differ, then that is not necessarily caused by serious differences in strategic interests and thinking, but often simply by the fact that the absence of a common functional strategy tempts the countries to resort to previously effective methods.

The aim of this article is not to offer a profound analysis of the relations between Russia and the West, or to draft a coherent blueprint for a new policy on Russia. Rather, it is an attempt to explore the position of the Nordic and Baltic countries and the Unites States within the framework of Russia's relations with the West, and to put forth some practical suggestions as to how the above mentioned nine countries can contribute to the forthcoming policy debates and improve the quality of the West's discussions on Russia and with Russia.

Moscow vis-à-vis the Hobbits and the Hegemon

At first glance, it may seem odd to perceive the Baltic-Nordic-U.S. group as an intellectual 'task force' for the formulation of a policy on Russia. When it comes to relations with Russia, what do these countries have in common, apart from the very general strategic interest shared by the whole Western community of seeing Russia become stable and democratic? The political weight categories, geographical locations, histories and, perhaps most importantly in this context, the images of these countries in the eyes of Moscow seem to differ drastically.

The Baltic-Nordic cluster of small dynamic countries is increasingly interconnected as a region, with criss-crossing trade and investment links, and promising co-operation projects in the spheres of energy security and hard security. The divide once imposed on the Baltic Sea by the Iron Curtain is decreasingly relevant and barely, if at all, noticeable. While the three Baltic states may still feel somewhat more vulnerable than others, all countries in the region share some Russia-related concerns and they all have significant stakes in Russia's stability and development.

However, from the Russian perspective, the old divide is still very much there. In the words of Dmitri Trenin, Moscow views the Nordic countries as prosperous and stable democracies and has learned to respect them, sometimes to admire them, and basically to trust them. The Baltic states, by contrast, are seen as former provinces who are still ungrateful to Moscow for graciously freeing them in 1991. Moscow regards them with deep suspicion, assuming that there are anti-Russian motives behind many of their actions and believing that they form a vocal anti-Russian lobby inside NATO and the EU.[1] While the Nordic countries are viewed as a potential source of investments and technological modernization, Moscow's agenda with the Baltic states is still largely overshadowed by emotional issues stemming from the past.

The experience of the past 20 years demonstrates that the Russian-Baltic link also serves as a sensitive indicator of the overall health of Russia's affinity with the West. Although Russia's relations with the Baltic states have always been complicated, they have shown signs of improvement when Russia has been striving for a generally co-operative arrangement with the West. But during Moscow's antagonistic and aggressive periods (e.g. during Putin's second term when Russia assumed it could dictate its terms to the West), the post-Soviet pro-Western neighbors have been the first to feel the heat.

However, for Russia, the Nordic and Baltic countries are united by their size. Size matters to Moscow. The Kremlin finds it very hard to fruitfully engage in Baltic-Nordic regional cooperation or, for that

---

[1] Dmitri Trenin, "Russian Policies towards the Nordic-Baltic Region", in Robert Nurick& Magnus Nordenman (eds.), *Nordic-Baltic Security in the 21st Century*, Atlantic Council, 2011, p. 47.

matter, in any other postmodern multilateral arrangement, such as with the EU. Its focus is on bilateral relations with large countries, and most important is the near-obsession with the Unites States. Russia demands that it be treated as a great power equal to the United States, notwithstanding Moscow's ability—or rather inability—to act as one. While Russia features fairly low on Washington's foreign policy agenda, the U.S. is always prominent in Russia's thoughts. In the past, this asymmetry in power and perception resulted in multiple emotional rows and there have even been some cases where Russia actually acted against its rational security interests with the sole aim of complicating the situation for the U.S.

It is interesting to point out that while Russia's attitude towards the Nordic countries can be characterized as fairly rational (at least by Moscow's standards), its attitude towards the Baltic countries and the United States, even though drastically different in its manifestations, has been shaped and defined by the very same factors—the loss of its empire and superpower status—which is why there is a strong emotional component. When the going is good, rational and interest-driven policies compete with emotions; when the going gets tough, both the Baltic states and the United States find themselves on the receiving end of Russia's frustration.

So, it appears that the Baltic and Nordic states and the U.S. actually have more in common than one might think in their debates on Russia. The Baltic and Nordic countries are similar in terms of their size, geographical location and security interests, but Russia views them from a drastically different perspective. The U.S. is set apart by its size, location and more complex security interests, but Russia's attitude towards it is shaped by the same factors as those affecting the Baltic states. This assortment of commonalities and differences should result in a variety of perspectives and experiences, the combination of which could lead to some potentially illuminating insights and policy ideas.

In the Beginning There Must Be Thoughts and Words

To start with, any good policy must proceed from analysis and discussion. The West's debates on Russia have not always lived up to high standards. At different times and places, they have suffered from political partisanship, almost compulsory preconceptions and taboo topics. Now things are changing: the combination of Russia's 2008 war with Georgia, Putin's return to the presidency, and the protests in society have removed the taboos and shaken the frozen conceptions. This transforming situation provides new perspectives and ample material for discussion.

However, even against a previously bleak background, the Baltic-Nordic community and the U.S. have always stood out as brighter spots. The lively think-tank scene in Washington may include some heavily partisan citadels, but it still always offers informed debates. The Nordic-Baltic region can boast a number of conferences that inspire frank discussions on a wide range of issues, including Russia: one can name the Lennart Meri Conference in Estonia, the Riga Conference in Latvia, the Snow Summit in Lithuania, the Visby Conference in Sweden and the European Business Leaders Convention in Finland. As probably any one of the organizers would testify, it is much easier to attract and invite prominent Americans to these conferences than people of equal status from large European countries. Whatever the reasons are behind this trend (is it the more competitive environment in America and the resulting higher intellectual curiosity of Americans, or the fact that superpowers need to reach out to their followers, or the legacy of the strategic debates held in the 1990s on NATO enlargement?), by now it has resulted in the creation of a Nordic-Baltic-U.S. policy community: a big, loose and lively group of politicians, experts, and civil servants from the above mentioned countries (and some additions from elsewhere); people who know one another and among whom policy debates and policy-plotting take place. This is something that already puts us in an advantaged position when it comes to devising a policy on Russia.

But we should strive to enlarge this community and to engage other strategically forward-thinking countries in Europe. With Poland already largely involved, this means most notably Germany, where an internal revolution in foreign-policy thinking is taking place, making the country more active and bringing it closer to the leadership position expected from it in Europe.

The upcoming debates on Russia should proceed on different levels and in different directions simultaneously. First, it is of course necessary to observe the foreign policy direction adopted by Putin and the day-to-day developments in Russian society and to devise appropriate policy responses. It is never easy for Western democracies to handle relations with authoritarian governments that face pro-democracy protests at home. In Russia's case, it will be aggravated by the fact that a large part of its leadership is obsessed with the West, assuming that the U.S. is an omnipotent meddler in the affairs of other countries and suspecting that the West has a hand in every social upheaval. At the same time, most of the protesters do not really care about the West— they see it neither as a role model nor as a source of all evil. The West does not really figure on their agenda. This means that any messages the Western countries might send risk not only being lost in society, but met with a hypersensitive suspicion in the circles close to the Kremlin.

But, in addition to the day-to-day management of the relations, we should also initiate debates on other levels. First, given the potentially historical implications of the processes currently underway in Russia, a few in-depth historical perspectives offered by academics would be of great interest.

Secondly, among senior civil servants and experts, it would be helpful to analyse our own recent policies vis-à-vis Russia. This should be undertaken by people with considerable inside knowledge aiming to analyze what has worked and what has made it work. Our interactions with Russia often lead to frustration, but there have also been some successes. So far, however, we have not managed to learn from those to create a coherent approach on that basis. Rather, sometimes our reaction to success has been fear, an instinct to think that 'we have pressured Russia so much, now we must give it something in return.' We should do the opposite—whenever we manage to defend our principles, we should try to learn from it and perpetuate it.

Thirdly, a similar discussion on the 'lessons learned' could be conducted with the participation of Nordic, Baltic and U.S. business people who have experiences in Russia, from the smallest companies to the largest. The comparison of experiences would help us learn and devise strategies and to form mutually beneficial relationships.

Fourth, we should discuss our own 'formative' experiences—the foreign policy strategies or failures from the past that provide the groundwork for our 'natural instincts' today. Estonia and Finland offer good examples here. The two countries analyze Russia in an almost identical manner, but their policy prescriptions differ a great deal, and often emotionally so. The Finns are convinced that Estonia's vocal criticism of Russia is childish and the Estonians are positive that the Finns' self-restraint is nothing but cowardly. In fact, self-restraint helped the Finns to preserve their country, or at least that is the dominant view. The Estonians tried self-restraint in 1939 and this led to a catastrophe. Estonia's independence came when everyone started speaking their minds. Most Estonian politicians have matured during the *perestroika* and *glasnost* years, but the essence of *glasnost* was to call a spade a spade over and over again until exhaustion. That is behind the Estonians' instinct to be vocal. So, both countries actually rely on the behavior that is perceived to have been successful in the past.

An alternative example is Germany's insistence on engagement with Russia which may sound a meaningless mantra when unskilfully delivered by bureaucrats, but acquires a different meaning if you take into account West Germany's courtship of East Germany with its perceived ultimate result of unification.

Knowing and emphatically feeling these backgrounds would help us to better understand the 'political personas' in our own community. It would increase mutual trust, help eliminate the divisive potential of the 'Russia issue' and contribute to the creation of a more cohesive community and to sounder policymaking.

Strategic Issues

When asked by this author what the EU's Russia policy should be, one of the continent's most brilliant minds thought for a moment and said: "We should take care of our energy security. And keep an eye on Ukraine. And that's basically it."[2] Maybe the interviewee could have added "doing our best to make sure that institutions or firms of Western countries do not engage in corrupt practices," but the point remains that effectively all we can do for Russia is keep our own house in order.

---

[2] Private conversation, March 2012.

We can do very little to influence Russia's strategic direction. Historically the latter has been influenced by huge territory, ill-defined borders that no buffer zone can secure properly, economic backwardness, an instinct to prefer absolutism to modernization and progress at critical junctions of history, and a fragmented national and torn cultural identity.[3] Nowadays Russia is engaged in a long transition—it has psychologically only just emerged from the collapse of the Soviet Union, and in the coming years it most likely will have to redefine its place in the world yet again, thanks to demographic trends, developments in the north Caucasus, and the rise of China. Russia knows neither what kind of a country it is now, nor what it will be in twenty years. Effectively, that means Russia also cannot have a well-defined and workable set of national interests. In this situation, its foreign policy becomes susceptible to circumstantial use; it can be guided or taken over by a vast array of agents, ranging from sophisticated philosophical conceptions to business interests of different clans and personalities, or as is most often the case, several things combined. This author has compared Russia's foreign policy to a Lego set, where the same pieces can be combined to create different outcomes. Other people have made the same comparison using the metaphor of a kaleidoscope.[4] Often Russia simply tries to maximize its influence so that it can be used at a later date as it sees fit; it tries to gain leverage, but not to use it—a behaviour that can actually be considered rational, given the circumstances, but makes life hard for those who are seriously seeking Russia's support in solving different strategic questions.

Ultimately, Russia's foreign policy can become sustainably coherent only once the existential and identity questions have been answered, at least for a time. That can only be done by the Russians themselves. All that the outsiders, including the West, can do, is provide as calm and law-based an outside environment as possible, which involves taking care of energy security and corruption and 'keeping an eye' on Ukraine and Georgia. Here, the Baltic and Nordic states along with the U.S. have an important role to play, but as both energy security

---

[3] As nicely summed up by Robert Legvold in "Past and Present in Russian Foreign Policy," in *Russia Lost or Found?*, published by Ministry of Foreign Affairs of Finland and Edita Publishing Ltd, Helsinki, 2009, p. 30–31.

[4] Ibid.

and the issues of 'Europe whole and free' are covered in other chapters of this publication, they are not dealt with here.

Engaging Unofficial Russia

Reaching out to Russian civil society is likely to be a dominant theme in policy discussions and policy-making in the West over the coming years.

In this context, it might be profitable for the Nordic-Baltic countries and for the U.S. to organize an informal 'donors' conference' and to make a list of what kind of assistance we have to offer. Our support might politically be less problematic and sometimes potentially also more effective if it is provided as shared experiences rather than as donations. But many good causes still need money, which is why we should explore various options for the establishment of a transparent and foolproof system for handling financial support, so as not to attract unsuitable applicants and not to give the Kremlin too convenient a pretext for harassing worthy applicants.

It is crucial to keep in mind that any form of civic activism—not just political—is commendable and deserves support. Support should not be limited to official NGOs, but should also involve other institutions: schools, health care institutions and official environmental organizations etc. which may also pursue worthy initiatives, creative approaches and self-sacrificial work ethics.

If the Nordic-Baltic countries and the U.S. combine their forces, they should, in theory, have a great deal of relevant experience to offer. The Nordic countries and the U.S. are likely to have prominent, established, and experienced NGOs that organize their activities at a much more advanced level than their counterparts in the Baltic states. The U.S., in particular, would probably have the know-how specific to a large nation. For example, the author of this article was once treated to a lecture at an NGO in Texas on how to keep track of the health records of migrant workers—something which yields little interest for Estonia, but which organizations in Russia might find very highly useful.

In the Baltic states, civic activism has occurred in two waves in the recent past: for the first time, in the late 1980s when it started out as an environmental or architectural heritage protection movement, but acquired a subversive anti-Soviet function by implication; and for the second time, in the early 21st century when, after having devoted a decade to working and earning money, people suddenly realized that individual wealth was not enough and that they as citizens had to fight for the common good, for public space, and for other causes. In today's Russia, both of the phases—subversive and responsibility-driven—are occurring simultaneously, which makes the experiences of the Baltic states more than relevant.

But Russian civil society could also be engaged to have—with any luck—a more immediate impact on not just domestic, but foreign policy debates in the country. In most countries, foreign policy tends to be a domain for the elites, with the general public having rather crude notions about this field. In Russia, however, there is a shortage of understanding even among such elites. Members of the elite can juggle with facts, but there are not many experts who actually understand the foreign policy thinking of the West. Mercantile colonialist ambitions are ascribed to most actions, especially those by the United States. Russian liberals who condemn the Kremlin's activities at home are often ready to uncritically accept the anti-liberal rhetoric of the Kremlin in foreign policy.

There are several possibilities open to the Nordic-Baltic countries and the U.S. to try to remedy the situation. For example, they could develop and fund initiatives for the development of a liberal view on foreign policy in Russia—such as an attempt made some time ago by the Liberal Mission Foundation which bore excellent fruit.[5]

Secondly, our embassies in Moscow could start informal but regular meetings, possibly at several levels simultaneously, with a two-fold goal: first, to discuss the current events among themselves, but secondly, to try to identify and engage some liberal-minded Russian foreign policy journalists or bloggers and to offer themselves as available sources of information to the latter. The objective should be to break through the propaganda filters imposed by state television and to get the Western version of events out there to the Russian blogosphere.

---

[5] See *"Rossiya i Zapad. Vneshnyaya politika Kremlya glazami liberalov"* ("Russia and the West. The Kremlin's Foreign Policy through the Eyes of Liberals"), Foundation Liberalnaya Missiya, Moscow, 2009,http://www.liberal.ru/articles/cat/1973.

This task cannot effectively be handled through bureaucratic and institutional channels; countless trips organized for Russian journalists by the State Department or the NATO Public Diplomacy Division are likely to result in a few polite and a few ironic articles in the Russian media, and nothing more. But multiple trusted and personally known sources who give credible information on a more or less permanent basis could bring different results. Furthermore, we should not aim to have a common message—we should also expose Russians to our debates to help them really understand our mentality.

Of course, for diplomats, this would mean unorthodox behavior. Then again, the activity of the current U.S. Ambassador Michael McFaul on Russian Twitter is already unorthodox. It might be beneficial if some of his Baltic and Nordic colleagues were willing to offer him some company on the social media scene and engage in discussions in full view of the Russian Internet. Social media would also provide an excellent venue for setting the record straight if someone from one of our countries is misquoted in the Russian mainstream media—knowingly, as often happens, or otherwise.

However, we should avoid the extremes—making social media compulsory for diplomats is not a good idea. Presence in the social media only works if one feels comfortable in the environment and if one dares to come out with some real messages and thoughts; tweeting thinly veiled PR messages is likely to be counterproductive.

Countering Official Russia

Tackling the Russian propaganda machine actually amounts to a strategic, rather than trivial, goal. When we hear Russian officials utter harsh words about the West or some neighboring country, we often dismiss them as directed to the domestic audience. This attitude is misguided. First, this rhetoric has for years also shaped the views of the domestic audience, reproducing those same attitudes, later to be diluted by the message that it was meant for the 'domestic audience.' (One cannot help but smile when seeing how it has finally caused a backlash against the Kremlin who these days need to explain to the Communists in Ulyanovsk that the erection of a NATO transit base does not actually mean military occupation of Russia.)

Secondly, it distorts and complicates debates among the Western allies. While bigger and more secure countries may dismiss aggressive statements as domestic propaganda, smaller and less secure countries cannot afford to do so, especially if they happen to be the targets of such statements; the result is another debate over the extent of the 'Russian threat' in the EU or NATO.

And thirdly, national leaders ought to explain their views to their domestic audiences. Living in a dual reality—the West is good when cooperation is required; the West is evil when culprits are sought—is something Orwellian and it definitely does not contribute to the development of Russia, nor does it facilitate Russia's relationship with the West. At the same time, Russian sociologists have labelled this kind of use of enemy figures as an integral part of the current Russian system. In the absence of normal legitimizing institutions—such as free elections and functioning institutions—those who are in power use enemy figures to mobilize apathetic audiences. "Running the country as if in a permanent state of emergency" was identified by the late Yuri Levada as one of the legacies of Stalinism, the others being the lack of functioning institutions and an inability to find a place in the world without permanently threatening others.[6]

Hence it would be beneficial if the Baltic and Nordic countries set themselves the goal of trying to make Russia responsible for its words by enquiring about its statements, by following up on them, by bringing the statements of lower officials up to higher levels by asking questions—publicly, if needed—and by pointing out inconsistencies.

But it must be understood that this is not just a foreign policy issue. By starting to fight the cynical uses of propaganda, we actually engage in nothing less than a struggle to transform the Russian state from a post-Stalinist one into a modern one.

---

[6] Yuri Levada, '*Osmyslit kult Stalina*,' ('To come to terms with the cult of Stalin') in *Stalinskie alternativy*, Moscow, Progress, 1989, p. 448–459.

Section IV

Energy Security

Chapter Eleven

Energy Security:
The Euro-Atlantic Community
and the Nordic-Baltic States

Matthew Bryza

For NATO and the EU, energy security means obtaining reliable, commercially viable, and environmentally sound supplies of oil, natural gas, and electricity at market-based prices without paying a political premium that undermines other strategic objectives such as European integration, as well as the political and economic freedom of EU members and partners across Eurasia. The Nordic and Baltic States (including Poland) can play a significant role in achieving these shared objectives, particularly with regard to natural gas and electricity, by:

- Catalyzing development of a more liquid natural gas market in Europe;

- Eliminating "energy islands" in the Baltic States to advance a Europe that is whole and free;

- Pulling Ukraine toward more transparent and market-based behavior on natural gas transit, and thereby, closer to Europe; and

- Nudging Gazprom toward more market-based behavior and more constructive relations with European consumers, Caspian exporters, and independent Russian gas producers.

Ambassador Matthew Bryza is Director of the International Center for Defence Studies in Tallinn and Non-Resident Senior Fellow at the Atlantic Council. He served as the deputy to the Special Advisor to the President and Secretary of State on Caspian Basin Energy Diplomacy from July 1998 to March 2001.

Europe's Non-Market Gas Market

In today's Europe, natural gas plays a more strategic role than any other fuel. This is because of the long-term nature of relationships between the producers and consumers of gas, given the large scale of natural gas infrastructure projects. Unlike oil, natural gas cannot simply be loaded onto tankers at the port nearest the wellhead for shipment around the globe. Given present technologies, natural gas can be transported in only two ways: via pipeline from the wellhead to the consumer, or via tanker only after having been liquefied. Pipelines and liquefaction plants both require billions of dollars of investment. To secure such high levels of financing, natural gas producers have traditionally preferred long-term contracts that provide security of demand in the form of consuming countries' commitment to purchase gas for 20 or even 25 years on a take-or-pay basis, (meaning purchasers must pay for the gas whether or not they ultimately take it) with the price of gas pegged to the price of oil.

As a result of such long-term contractual arrangements, Europe's natural gas market is far from an actual market. Pricing is determined less by market forces of supply and demand than by suppliers who insist on pegging the purchase price of their gas to the price of oil. While good for gas producers, who lock in customers at higher prices than in a competitive market for gas, this approach has not always been good for European consumers; it has retarded development of gas-on-gas competition in Europe, which, if allowed to flourish as in the United States, should lead to significantly lower gas prices for European consumers. Excess supply, due to the rapid expansion of shale gas production, coupled with trading in the world's most liquid and competitive market, result in U.S. natural gas prices that are only one-fifth of those in Europe.

European leaders have been willing to lock themselves into long-term agreements with Gazprom (and other gas producers) in order to avoid politically disastrous gas shortages in winter. Consequently, many European countries find themselves heavily dependent on Gazprom, Russia's national champion, who provides 25% of all the gas Europe consumes, and 80% to 100% of the gas consumed in northeastern and southeastern Europe. The Baltic States rely entirely on Soviet-era pipelines to deliver gas from western Siberia. Lacking gas interconnections with the rest of Europe, the three Baltic States constitute an "energy island" within the EU.

Russian political leaders have, at times, exploited European fears of gas cutoffs to strengthen Gazprom's monopolistic power. For example, during peak winter cold spells in 2006 and 2009, Gazprom cut off natural gas flows to Europe via Ukraine, in violation of its contractual commitments to supply gas to EU customers. Granted, Ukraine's own non-transparent behavior provided genuine grounds for disagreement. But, these disputes were about more than the cost of transiting and purchasing gas in Ukraine; in both cases, Gazprom demanded acquisition and/or control of Ukraine's natural gas pipelines and storage facilities as a condition for resuming gas flows to both Ukrainian and EU customers. This type of demand underscores a deeper Russian motive of preserving Gazprom's monopolistic power on gas imports into Europe, which Ukraine had been undercutting through tough bargaining tactics on transit tariffs and purchase prices for Russian gas. As a result, European consumers suffered.

Similarly, when another serious cold spell enveloped Europe in February 2012, Gazprom claimed it had no choice but to allow more of its gas to be consumed in Russia, leaving less to be exported to Europe. This marked another violation of Gazprom's contractual obligations to European consumers. Gazprom could have pumped additional gas from Turkmenistan to Europe. The Russian company was in fact legally required to do so, based on its existing take-or-pay gas contract with Turkmenistan, of which it has been in breach after refusing since 2009 to purchase its contracted volume of gas from Turkmenistan and shutting down the Turkmenistan-Russia pipeline. (This unannounced and uncoordinated shutdown caused an explosion that rendered the pipeline inoperable, which Gazprom then argued, released it from its take-or-pay commitment to Turkmenistan.) Thus, instead of honoring its contractual obligations with both Turkmenistani gas producers and European consumers, Gazprom again chose to allow European consumers to suffer.

Amazingly, during this same period of cold weather, Gazprom chose to send more gas to Turkey. While Turkey had not agreed to pay more for this Russian gas, it had recently agreed to permit the construction of Gazprom's massive new pipeline, South Stream, in its

Black Sea territorial waters. This mammoth undersea pipeline will help Gazprom shore up its monopolistic positions in Europe by bypassing Ukraine and undercutting European efforts to develop a southern corridor of gas pipelines from Azerbaijan that Gazprom could not control. Hence, by cutting gas to the EU while increasing flows to Turkey, Russia signaled that it may not be as reliable a supplier to those who facilitate competition with Gazprom.

Efforts by the Russian government and Gazprom to isolate Ukraine and undercut the southern corridor are two elements of a single strategy to stifle competition and thereby sustain Gazprom's monopolistic power in Europe. For decades, Gazprom's monopsonist/monopolist power has enabled it to buy natural gas in central Asia at a relatively low price and sell it in Europe at three times the purchase price. Such arrangements have generated enormous profits for Gazprom. The Russian company has therefore concentrated on sustaining its monopolistic power in three key ways: by trying to block competitive pipelines to Europe such as the southern corridor; by bypassing Ukraine, Poland, and the Baltic States through less commercially attractive mega-projects like South Stream; and by preventing access to Gazprom's pipeline network for independent Russian or central Asian gas producers. In keeping with monopolistic ambitions, Gazprom has also foregone other steps that a free-market company would take to maintain its competitiveness, such as developing more of its own gas fields in Russia, and building natural gas storage facilities that are essential to meet peak consumer demand during the winter. Gazprom has consequently undercut its ability to meet its gas supply commitments to European consumers during peak winter cold.

In summary, the above Gazprom/Russian approach generates three strategically significant consequences for Europe:

- European consumers pay more for natural gas and enjoy less security of supply than would be the case in a truly competative market;

- Reemergence of a Europe that is whole and free is slowed; and

- Russia's own natural gas industry remains underdeveloped and under-competitive.

Market Forces and North Sea Gas Trading Hubs

The European Union has been working to counter these negative consequences for over a decade by pursuing the formation of a unified internal energy market by 2014. The EU's Third Energy Package, passed in 2009, aims to bolster the impact of market forces in determining the price of natural gas (and electricity). The Third Package mandates: unbundling of natural gas transit and distribution networks to reduce the monopoly power of national champion energy companies (whether Russian or European); financial support for new pipeline systems that can diversify sources of gas supply (such as the southern corridor) and connect gas grids across Europe; support for the expansion of gas trading hubs; integrating gas storage facilities into gas trading hubs; and connectivity of Baltic electricity networks with those of Nordic countries, Poland, and the EU.

Perhaps the most significant of the above factors is the expansion of gas trading hubs. Hubs are places where major gas pipelines meet and where a market forms, with buyers and sellers bargaining over competing supplies of natural gas. Prices at hubs are set according to gas-on-gas competition rather than by oil prices. In the long run, Europe will maximize its energy security as natural gas markets grow more efficient through hub-based trading, since efficient markets maximize security of supply and demand at fair prices without political interference.

The market efficiency of a hub depends on its liquidity—i.e., the degree to which a single gas trade can occur without affecting the price of subsequent trades. Liquidity at a hub requires several factors: access to diversified gas supplies through the convergence of pipelines and/or liquid natural gas terminals somewhere nearby; gas storage facilities to manage peak demand in winter and minimal demand in summer; and connectivity to consumers via pipelines and trading regulations. The best example in the world is Henry Hub in the United States, where a range of independent gas suppliers can store their gas, trade it freely, and deliver it to customers based on price signals set by supply and demand.

The world's second most liquid natural gas hub is the UK's National Balancing Point (NBP), which was created when the British government privatized British Gas in December 1986 and mandated the company to release gas volumes to independent suppliers. Other hubs are now emerging around the North Sea and competing with the NBP. These include the Title Transfer Facility (TTF) in the Netherlands, Zeebrugge in Belgium, PEG Nord in France, and NetConnect Germany (NCG) and Gaspool in Germany. All are competing to surpass NBP in liquidity and become Europe's primary gas trading hub, and trade gas produced in the UK, Norway, the Netherlands, and Russia. They face additional competition from the Central European Gas Hub (CEGH) in Baumgarten, Austria, located on the Austria-Slovakia border at the strategic juncture of Gazprom's major pipelines, which is also the possible endpoint of both the Nabucco and South Stream pipelines.

Each of these hubs is expanding its services beyond the physical transfer of gas to include storage, processing, and trading. As a result, the volume and liquidity of trading at these hubs is increasing rapidly. In 2011, for example, TTF nearly doubled the volume of gas traded, and now challenges the NBP as Europe's most liquid hub. Liquidity also increased during 2011 at all the other Northwestern European gas hubs, doubling at France's PEG Nord (according to the ICIS Heren Tradeability Index).

As liquidity has increased, nascent spot markets have emerged at these trading hubs, free from any connection to oil prices or manipulation by monopolists. Since 2008, (according to the Oxford Institute for Energy Studies), spot prices for natural gas at larger hubs in Northwestern Europe have achieved convergence. In other words, liberalized pricing is leading toward consolidation of trading at separate North Sea hubs into a single regional market, where supply and demand set prices according to gas-on-gas competition. Hence, the North Sea basin has emerged as a localized version of the unified natural gas market, which the EU seeks for all of Europe.

Expanding Trading Hubs Eastward

Perhaps the most efficient way for the EU to establish a unified market for natural gas is via the incremental spread of liberalized pricing and trading hubs beyond the North Sea. Price liberalization is indeed beginning make inroads into Germany and the Baltic Sea

Basin. This began in February 2010, when spot markets at North Sea gas hubs allowed TTF to extract Gazprom's agreement for spot pricing to account for 15% of its gas price at TTF. Germany's E.ON AG quickly followed, asking Gazprom to index fully its sales price under a long-term contract to spot prices for gas rather than the price of oil.

Gazprom refused to do so. Later that month, Poland's PGNiG and Lithuania's gas utility asked Gazprom to allow market-based pricing in their own long-term contracts. In the absence of market forces generated by gas trading hubs, Gazprom also rebuffed the Polish and Lithuanian requests. The Polish and Lithuanian entities responded by threatening to take Gazprom to arbitration. Gazprom Deputy CEO Aleksander Medvedev's response was chilling: "If it does come to arbitration proceedings, we are pretty confident.... God help them if someone takes a risk to go to arbitration."

Gazprom recognizes that the spread of spot pricing from the North Sea to the Baltic basin severely threatens monopolistic power in Europe. Gazprom will therefore fight hard to maintain the isolation of natural gas markets from the gas trading hubs emerging around the North Sea. That is indeed one of the objectives of the Nord Stream pipeline under the Baltic Sea, which connects Russia and Germany while bypassing the Baltics, Scandinavia, and Poland.

Facilitating the eastward spread of market-based gas trading into the Baltic Basin is the most significant step the Nordic States, Baltic States, and the rest of the EU can take to weaken Gazprom's monopoly power and strengthen Europe's energy security with respect to natural gas. Norway, in particular, can play a critical role. In recent decades, Norwegian natural gas, coupled with Netherlands- and UK-produced gas, has enabled North Sea gas trading hubs to emerge by providing alternative supplies that can compete with Gazprom's volumes. In the past year, Norway's new discoveries, including the landmark Johan Sverdrup oil and gas field on Norway's continental shelf, and the Norvarg and Skalle gas finds in the Barents Sea, could eventually provide the diversified supplies of gas needed to catalyze gas hubs in the Baltic basin, should Poland, the Baltic States, and their EU partners put in place the regulatory structures, inter-connections, and storage facilities required to expand the North Sea trading system to the Baltic basin.

Until now, the Baltic region has existed as an energy island. A single company, Gazprom, has been the region's predominant gas supplier for decades, providing 100% of Finland's and the Baltic States' natural gas. Gazprom has bolstered its leverage in the Baltic States by acquiring control of gas storage facilities in Latvia, and by bypassing the region with its Nord Stream pipeline. These efforts to isolate the Baltic States from their EU partners have largely worked, with the Baltic States' integration into the EU's emerging natural gas market remaining limited. The same is true with respect to electricity, as the Baltic States remain integrated into northwest Russia's electricity grid—as during the Soviet Union's existence—rather than into the EU grid. Moreover, the Baltic States' lack of energy integration into the EU hinders the achievement of one of the Euro-Atlantic community's most fundamental goals: completion of a Europe that is whole and free.

Estonia, Latvia, and Lithuania have failed to develop a coordinated approach with each other and with Poland, (their gateway to EU integration), on strategic energy issues. Individually, however, they are developing new energy infrastructure that could comprise the components of regional markets for natural gas and electricity, which could facilitate their deeper integration into the EU. On gas, Latvia has modernized and expanded its natural gas storage facilities. However, this has occurred in cooperation with Gazprom rather than with its Baltic neighbors. Lithuania is procuring a floating liquid natural gas re-gasification facility at Klaipeda with a capacity of 2 to 3 BCM to begin operation in 2014, but without a plan to use this diversified source of supply to catalyze development of a regional trading system that could emerge into a localized gas hub. Poland is building a 5 BCM re-gasification plant at Swinoujscie also to begin operating in 2014. In addition, Poland is planning a 2.3 BCM gas pipeline to Lithuania, which could be expanded to 4.5 BCM, but apparently without a regional strategy to integrate either of these projects into a Baltic gas trading hub.

On electricity, Estonia connected its national grid with Finland's via the 350 MW Estlink cable in 2007. Both countries will expand this important connection via a new 659 MW cable in 2014. Connectivity between Nordic and Baltic electricity networks will be further strengthened in 2016 with the completion of the 650 MW NordBalt electricity cable between Sweden and Lithuania. Poland and Lithuania have been planning an electricity link for several years, but have failed to close the deal due to bickering over financing, electricity purchases from the replacement for the mothballed Ignalina nuclear power plant, and bilateral political issues. Lithuania is also angry with Brussels over reduced EU subsidies for construction of the replacement of the Ignalina nuclear plant, the closure of which was mandated by the EU. Finally, the three Baltic States have been unable to agree on a joint approach to synchronize their electricity grids with the EU's grid: Estonia and Lithuania are ready to move ahead, while Latvia prefers to forego the significant costs of European electricity integration and instead continue to rely on integration with the Northwest Russian grid.

The Baltic and Nordic states are thus putting into place the building blocks of a regional energy security strategy that supports the EU's goals of a liberalized natural gas market and integrated electricity grids among all its members. But, they are not integrating these measures into a joint plan. In the absence of a more coherent and coordinated approach, these countries on Europe's northeastern flank risk drifting for years on separate trajectories, without the concerted effort required to develop localized gas trading hubs and integrated electricity systems required in order to eliminate the Baltic "energy island."

Now is the right time for the Baltic and Nordic states, together with Poland, to develop a joint Baltic Basin Energy Market Strategy, which would define a vision for the emergence of natural gas trading hubs and integrated electricity grids among the Baltic basin and Nordic states, Poland, and other EU partners. The Nordic states and Poland would play three key roles in developing the requisite physical and regulatory infrastructure: geographic connectivity to the EU; political support within the EU (except for Norway); and sources of investment.

Baltic Natural Gas

Encourage emergence of Baltic gas trading hubs through joint policies and regulations.

- EU/ Norway encourage Baltic States to agree to develop a limited number of trading hubs.

- Baltic States advance hubs' evolution by coordinating regulatory regimes on:
  * Interstate sales of gas; and
  * De-congestion of interconnections (to free up gas transit capacity that utilities may book in advance but not ultimately use).

Facilitate growth of liquidity at Baltic hubs by securing diversified sources of gas supply.

- Baltics and other Nordics, with EU support, convince Norway/Statoil to market future Barents Sea natural gas in the Baltic basin.

- Poland and Lithuania complete construction of re-gasification facilities for LNG.

- Coordinate with Latvia to secure Riga's buy-in on gas storage (see below).

- EU encourages Poland's development of shale gas, which could significantly reduce the Baltic basin's dependence on Gazprom if geological expectations play out and infrastructure costs do not undercut shale gas' commerciality.

- If Gazprom seeks to undersell Polish shale gas, which will be more expensive to produce, EU customers may demand more market-based pricing.

- Poland prepares "gas release program" to provide gas to future hub.

- Poland and Lithuania advocate in the U.S. for potential LNG supplies.
  * Huge over-supply of natural gas in the U.S. due to shale gas provides incentive for U.S. exports.
  * But LNG exports face political obstacles in the U.S. from environmentalists and from politicians who fear LNG exports will raise domestic gas prices.
  * Europe must compete with Asia for North American LNG.

- EU and Norway encourage Russia to market a portion of future gas from the Shtokman and Bovanenko fields in the Baltic basin.

Increase liquidity at Baltic hubs via commercial access to Latvia's gas storage facilities.

- Baltics and European Commission seek joint venture (perhaps with Gazprom) to integrate Latvia's Gazprom-operated gas storage into hub-based gas trading system.

Increase liquidity at Baltic hubs by developing regional pipeline interconnections.

- EU offers political (and possible financial) support for gas inter-connection between Poland and Lithuania, and between Lithuania and Latvia.

Baltic Electricity

Increase Baltic power generation by completing replacement for Ignalina nuclear plant.

- EU and Lithuania resolve funding dispute over decommissioning of Ignalina 2, which shut down at end of 2009.

- Power companies of Lithuania, Estonia, Latvia, and Poland further develop investment plans, in cooperation with Hitachi, for 3200 MV replacement nuclear station at Visaginas, Lithuania.

Eliminate Baltic electricity island via electricity connections with Nordics and Poland.

- Estonia and Finland complete 650 MW Estlink 2 cable (2014).

- Lithuania and Sweden complete 750 MW NordBalt cable (2016).

- Lithuania and Poland complete 1000 KV LitPo cable (2015).

Strengthen Nordic-Baltic electricity market through regulatory reform.

- Develop regulatory structures to facilitate cross-border trade of Latvian hydropower, Estonian thermal power, future Lithuanian nuclear power, as well as Finnish and Swedish electricity, among all five countries.

Integrate with Europe by synchronizing Baltic electricity networks with the EU's grid.

- Estonia and Lithuania, in cooperation with the EU, develop incentives to convince Latvia to end synchronization with the northwest Russia grid.

Ukraine, Russia, and Baltic Hubs

Though Ukraine is not a littoral state of the Baltic Sea, its own behavior and its treatment by Russia can significantly influence whether the Baltic States establish the natural gas trading hub(s) at the heart of the aforementioned Baltic energy strategy.

Non-transparency in Ukraine's energy sector, especially Ukraine's confiscation of Russian gas transiting through its territory, led many Europeans to believe that Russia was justified in bypassing Ukraine (along with the Baltic States and Poland) by building the Nord Stream pipeline under the Baltic Sea. Though Gazprom's German, French, and Dutch partners may have recognized that Russia aimed at least in part to use the Nord Stream to obtain the political objective of slowing Ukraine's integration into Europe, they also realized that receiving Russian gas via a dedicated pipeline was cheaper and more reliable than gas transit via Ukraine. Now in full operation and set to expand, Nord Stream will compete to ship to Europe not only future volumes of Russian gas, but Norwegian gas as well that might otherwise help launch crucially important gas trading hubs in the Baltic Sea Basin.

However, the EU can attract some of that future Norwegian gas, and maybe even some Russian gas, to a Baltic basin market. While responsibility will lie primarily with the Baltic States, Ukraine can also play a significant role by eliminating the pretext for Russia and its European partners to bypass both Ukraine and the Baltic. This will require Ukraine to work cooperatively and more transparently with both Russia and the EU on gas transit.

EU cajoling alone will not suffice to solicit this monumental shift in behavior by Ukraine's energy actors. The EU should consider developing a commercial vehicle to expand the capacity of Ukraine's gas transit system by 10 to 20 BCM through a joint EU-Russian investment in de-bottlenecking transit pipelines in southwestern Ukraine that lead to Slovakia and the rest of the EU. In exchange, Ukraine would agree to strict monitoring by the EU and Russia of the operation of its gas transit system (to prevent theft of Russian gas) and to reasonable transit fees. Germany proposed a similar approach nearly a decade ago. The U.S. and EU expressed support for such a collaborative effort among the EU, Ukraine, and Russia in the final line of the communiqué for the June 2009 U.S.-EU Summit. Progress subsequently stalled as Ukrainian politics descended into its current state of crisis.

Looking ahead to a period when Ukrainian politics will have settled, such an EU-Ukraine-Russia joint venture could catalyze several important strategic developments related to European energy security. First, this approach would help Ukraine rebuild its reputation as a worthy European partner on energy security, and thereby restore enthusiasm for Ukraine's deeper integration into Europe. Second, an expanded and reliable Ukrainian gas transit network could change the psychological-commercial dynamic that currently drives Norwegian gas producers and Northern European consumers to rely on the Nord Stream pipeline, rather than exploring cheaper land-based transit options that embrace the Baltic States and Poland. Attracting some Norwegian gas to Europe's Northeastern flank, and building gas interconnections among three Baltic States, could catalyze development of gas trading hubs in the Baltic Basin. Connecting these gas networks with Poland's pipelines, and then with Ukraine's, could facilitate the convergence of spot prices for gas; the key precondition for a unified European gas market.

Besides Ukraine, the Baltic States, and the rest of the EU, Russia would also benefit from this approach over time. The expansion of gas trading hubs and spot market pricing will compel Gazprom to take key steps required to maintain its competitiveness in a European gas market in which prices are finally set by market forces. Such measures will include investment in gas storage and opening Gazprom's pipelines to independent Russian and central Asian producers. While Gazprom may be reluctant to undertake these sorts of prudent investments as long as its monopoly power allows it to extract rents from gas sales in Europe, these measures will eventually ensure Russia's long-term reliability as a supplier of natural gas to Europe; they will also maximize Gazprom's revenues once the rents it currently seeks are no longer available. Europeans would gain cheaper and more reliable gas supplies, plus a more sustainable partnership with Russia, based on shared economic interests. Russia would benefit from lower domestic gas prices and a national gas company that is more competitive and enjoys more credibility in capital markets.

Poland can have a major impact on all of the above developments. Given its special relationship with Ukraine and its status within the European Union, Poland can play a key role in brokering agreement among Ukraine, Russia, and the EU to develop such a commercial venture. Furthermore, the development of Poland's shale gas resources, if proven commercial, could provide a major new supply of natural gas that could catalyze the development of gas trading hubs in the Baltic basin.

The European Union will take the lead role among Euro-Atlantic institutions in implementing the full range of measures outlined in this paper. But NATO can also play an important part by highlighting in its NAC deliberations and ministerial/summit communiqués the geopolitical importance of supporting the EU in achieving a unified European energy market that enables the reemergence of a Europe that is whole and free, especially with regard to the Baltic States.

Chapter Twelve

Transatlantic Dimension of Energy Security in the Baltic Sea Region

Andris Sprūds

Energy security is one of the central themes on the transatlantic agenda. Structural and perceptual differences, however, exist within the transatlantic community. The Baltic Sea region gradually emerges, increasingly consolidated, and as one of the most dynamic regions in the transatlantic area. At the same time, the internal regional imbalances and complexities in energy supply, market, and transit patterns remain; a number of major energy projects are expected to address those challenges. Moreover, developments in the energy sector in the Baltic Sea region have become a "stress test" for a wider strategic interaction among NATO, EU and Russia. This raises the question of whether and how national energy responses and ambitious regional initiatives would contribute to a transforming energy configuration of the Baltic Sea region and the nature of the prospective transatlantic dimension of the regional energy security quest.

Regional Energy Diversity

During the last twenty years, the Baltic Sea region has undergone a fundamental transformation. The enlargement of the Euro-Atlantic institutions has been accompanied by a number of endeavors and ini-

Dr. Andris Sprūds is Director of Latvian Institute of International Affairs. He also holds a position of professor at Riga Stradins University and adiunkt at Wyzsza Szkola Biznesu-National Louis University in Nowy Sacz, Poland. Andris Spruds has been a visiting student and scholar at Oxford, Uppsala, Columbia University as well as Norwegian Institute of International Affairs and Japan's Institute of Energy Economics. He was also a Fulbright Fellow at the Center for Transatlantic Relations at Johns Hopkins University. Andris Spruds is a board member of Latvian Transatlantic organization and Baltic-Black Sea Alliance.

tiatives to institutionalize regional cooperation, including collaboration in the energy sector. Essentially, EU-ization of the Baltic Sea region has occurred. The region was also the first to adopt an internal EU regional strategy in 2009 with a strong commitment to further integrate the regional energy infrastructure and promote efficiency and security of energy markets.[1]

A significant number of regional energy initiatives notwithstanding, a comprehensive and effective regional energy architecture or institutional framework is still absent. The existing organizations represent a variety of institutions differing in their objectives, scope, efficiency, and political and financial capacity.[2] The somewhat inconsistent institutional contraption in the region has been the outcome of various sub-regional processes as well as national governments' approaches to, and perceptions of, security of supply, liberalization and sustainable energy. As a result, a multi-layer Baltic-Nordic energy architecture has essentially come into existence in terms of institutional integration and cooperation.[3]

The five Nordic countries[4] form the core of the region. They have a long tradition of cooperation through the Nordic Council and Nordic Council of Ministers. The Nordic countries closely cooperate on a variety of energy issues, have created an integrated Nordic electricity system and Nord Pool electricity market, and actively promote the sustainable energy agenda internationally. In addition to the Baltic

---

[1] European Commission, Communication the Concerning European Union Strategy for the Baltic Sea Region, COM (2009) 248, 6 June 2009; Action Plan: working document accompanying the Communication concerning the European Union Strategy for the Baltic Sea Region—SEC(2009) 712, 6 June 2009, updated December 2010.

[2] The Council of Baltic Sea States has been a primary umbrella organization for a number of initiatives: Baltic Sea Energy Co-operation (BASREC), Joint Energy and Climate Platform of Baltic Sea Region Organizations, Baltic 21 (a network of governmental and nongovernmental organizations to promote sustainable development), Baltrel (Baltic Ring Electricity Co-operation Committee representing electricity companies), Baltic Gas (an association representing gas transmission companies), and others.

[3] Andris Spruds, "Energy and Regional Cooperation: towards the Baltic Energy Rim?" in Robert Nurick and Magnus Nordenman (eds.), *Nordic-Baltic Security in the 21st Century: the Regional Agenda and the Global Role* (Washington, DC: Atlantic Council, 2011), pp. 35–40.

[4] Denmark, Finland, Iceland, Norway, and Sweden.

Sea regional institutions, the Nordic countries are engaged in the Arctic Council and Barents Euro-Atlantic Council (except Denmark and Iceland). Finland successfully initiated the Northern Dimension in 1999 and the refurbished Northern Dimension policy in 2006 with an aim to promote cooperation and joint projects, with Russia adopting a "small-but-smart" and "fly-below-the-radar" approach.[5]

Germany, Poland, and the Baltic countries form another layer of the countries in the Baltic Sea. All of them belong to Euro-Atlantic institutions but their varying size, location and background has also contributed to policy priority differences. Although Germany and Poland have considerable interest in cooperating in the Baltic Sea region, both countries have a number of regional and wider transatlantic agendas. For instance, Poland has cooperated actively on energy issues in the framework of the Visegrad Group.[6] The three Baltic countries have prioritized the regional integration of their energy markets. However, the Soviet legacy left considerable institutional, regulatory, infrastructural and financial obstacles to overcome. The important step of integrating the Baltic "energy island" into the regional, and above all Nordic, markets has been adopted in the EU Strategy for the Baltic Sea Region and in its integral part, namely, the Baltic Energy Market Interconnection Plan (BEMIP) in June 2009.[7]

Even more significantly, national energy mixes, perceptions and strategies across the region vary considerably due to nationally-specific energy production, established supply routes and infrastructure or particular economic and political preferences. In this regard, the Baltic Sea countries may be divided into several groups in terms of secure and competitive supplies as well as perceptions of and implemented policy regarding "energy security" and "overdependence" on imported resources.

---

[5] Pami Aalto, Helge Blakkisrud and Hanna Smith (eds.), *The New Northern Dimension of the European Neighbourhood* (Brussels: CEPS, 2008).

[6] The Visegrad Group convened Energy Security Summit in Budapest in February 2010 with participation of the countries from Central and South Europe as well as US, EC and IEA; see, Ernest Wyciszkiewicz, "Energy Summit in Budapest," *Bulletin of the Polish Institute of International Affairs*, 5 March 2010.

[7] Memorandum of Understanding on the Baltic Energy Market Interconnection Plan, 17 June 2009; for more information see: http://ec.europa.eu/energy/infrastructure/bemip_en.htm.

Among the members of the Euro-Atlantic community, Norway is one of the major regional suppliers, and its energy security is primarily perceived in terms of security of demand. Germany, Denmark, Sweden, and Poland are reliant on and, respectively, sensitive to external supplies. However, these countries have developed considerable domestic production and generation capacities and have their own "national champions." Moreover, these countries have achieved progress in terms of supply diversification. This partly compensates for their reliance on imported energy and allows its energy security to be interpreted largely in economic and environmental, rather than political, terms. Poland's example has been indicative in transforming the country's previously strongly securitized energy strategy, exemplified by the proposed idea of energy NATO, to a more de-securitized approach.[8]

The Baltic countries and, partly, Finland constitute an "energy island" within the Euro-Atlantic community. Finland and Estonia, however, differ from their southern neighbours in some important aspects. Finland has been actively developing its own nuclear generation capacity, has electricity interconnections with its Scandinavian neighbours and participates in the common Nordic electricity market. Finland also views cooperation with Russia as an economic opportunity rather than a political risk. Estonia has been a frontrunner among the Baltic countries to proceed with integration into the Nordic electricity market by building interconnections and adopting the relevant regulatory and legislative norms. Estonia domestically ensures around two thirds of its energy requirements relying on its wood, peat, and especially, oil shale production. Estonia is the only country in the world which ensures power generation almost entirely from oil shale.[9] The country has even undertaken to promote its oil shale production expertise abroad and has acquired assets in Jordan and the U.S.

Latvia and Lithuania appear to be most reliant on imported resources, from, above all, Russia. While Russia's natural gas is esti-

---

[8] Poland's Ministry of Economics, Polityka energetyczna Polski do 2030 roku, adopted by the government on 10 November 2009, http://www.mg.gov.pl/files/upload/8134/Polityka%20energetyczna%20ost.pdf

[9] Merle Maigre, "Energy Security Concerns of the Baltic States," Analysis of the Estonian International Centre for Defence Studies, 2 March 2010, www.icds.ee

mated to account for around 7% of the EU's primary energy balance, it is more than 30% in the case of Latvia and even higher in Lithuania after the closure of the Ignalina nuclear power plant in 2009.[10] Gazprom is a dominant shareholder in both national gas distribution monopolies. Regardless of the political implications, a high reliance on a single supplier means potentially unfavorable price formations and almost non-existent alternatives in the case of technical problems such as gas disruptions. A limited infrastructure and supply capacity and market liquidity have placed the Baltic countries, especially Latvia and Lithuania, high on the so-called import vulnerability indexes, particularly when it comes to gas.[11] This has motivated both countries to frame their energy strategy priorities in terms of "energy independence," to diversify energy supplies away from Russia and to promote the transatlantic dimension of energy security.

Russia: an Indispensable Regional Energy Nation?

The launch of the Nord Stream gas pipeline in November 2011 demonstrated a continuous mutual interest and significance regarding energy supplies in Russia's interaction with the EU and its partners in the Baltic Sea region. The inauguration of the pipeline, however, also evoked controversy surrounding concerns among a number of the countries in the region regarding security of supply and the liberalization of energy markets. Russia's supplies of energy resources play an important role in the Baltic Sea region. Although Norway has become a substantial energy supplier to the countries in its proximity, Russia remains essentially an "indispensable energy nation." In the region, Russia delivers around half of all natural gas consumed. Russia's oil and gas account for the majority of Latvia's and Lithuania's primary energy balance. Although Estonia is a rather energy self-sufficient country, Russia secures Estonia's gas needs and a considerable share of its oil consumption. Similarly, Russia's energy resources feature sub-

---

[10]Sachi Findlater and Pierre Noel, "Gas Supply Security in the Baltic States: A Qualitative Assessment," Working Paper, University of Cambridge Electricity Policy Research Group, March 2010.

[11]Iana Dreyer, Fredrik Erixon, and Robert Winkler, "The Quest for Gas Market Competition: Fighting Europe's Dependency on Russian Gas more Effectively," European Centre for International Political Economy, Occasional Paper No. 1, 2010.

stantially in Finland's energy balance. Sweden, Poland, and Germany also rely considerably on Russian oil and gas imports. Russia's gas share in the energy balance of Germany may even increase further after German government decided to phase out its nuclear capacities following the Fukushima nuclear disaster.[12]

The backbone of the energy infrastructure in the Baltic Sea region relates mostly to Russia. The northern branch of the Druzhba oil pipeline delivers crude oil to Poland and Germany through Belarus. The shipments of the crude oil through pipeline branches to the Latvian port of Ventspils and the Lithuanian Butinge port and Mazeiku refinery ceased during the last decade and were redirected through the Baltic pipeline system to Russia's Primorsk port, and prospectively to Ust-Luga, in the Gulf of Finland. Over half of Russian crude oil exports are either transported to the countries in the region or through the region.[13] The Yamal-Europe pipeline delivers gas to Poland and Germany through Belarus, while the newly built Nord Stream will considerably strengthen the presence of Russian gas supply in the whole of Northern Europe. The electricity transmission system of Russia and the CIS extends into and integrates the three Baltic countries.

The regional security of supply debate has been primarily focused on natural gas supplies from Russia and on prospective diversification alternatives. However, more recently the regional configuration of electricity supplies, power generation facilities and interconnections has also become an important issue in the regional energy dynamics. Although the Lithuanian government has stated its continuous and firm intention to proceed with the construction of a nuclear power plant in Visagina, prospective nuclear power plants in Belarus, and especially in Russia's Kaliningrad region, may raise questions regarding the economic feasibility and complementarities of those projects.[14]

---

[12]Andris Sprūds, "Russia in the Baltic Sea Regional Energy Architecture" in Andres Kasekamp (ed.), *Estonian Foreign Policy Yearbook 2011* (Tallinn: Estonian Foreign Policy Institute, 2012).

[13]Peeter Vahtra and Stefan Ehrstedt, "Russian Energy Supplies and the Baltic Sea Region," Pan-European Institute of Turku School of Economics, Electronic Publication No. 14 (2008).

[14]Baltic Development Forum, Report, "Sustainable Energy Scenarios: Energy Perspectives for the Kaliningrad Region as an Integrated Part of the Baltic Sea Region," 2010.

Russia has demonstrated its willingness to retain a considerable presence in the electricity markets in the Baltic Sea region and to participate in the "nuclear power plant race," if necessary. The cooperative efforts of the three Baltic countries, EU-ization and further interconnections again may serve as the most appropriate response to the challenges of security of supply in the power generation sector.

Recent developments pinpoint that the debate about the security of supply has been complemented with a market liberalization and ownership unbundling issue. Essentially this has turned into a primary contentious item on the regional energy agenda, in general, and in relations with Russia and its gas monopoly Gazprom, in particular. Russia has primarily framed liberalization, in general, and its Third Energy Package, in particular, as instruments to preclude Gazprom from prospective investments and participation in European gas downstream business. It is also an attempt to reduce its current ownership stakes.

EU members have demonstrated a variety of policy responses in the process of liberalization. Considerable progress in terms of market liberalization has been achieved in the electricity sector. Competition in the gas sector, however, is more challenging to ensure due to its traditionally more monopolistic structure. Sweden and Denmark have adopted full ownership unbundling while Germany and apparently Poland are joining a number of the EU countries in preferring the third ITO (Independent Transmission Operator) option or the so-called "status quo plus" model. The ITO model requires ensuring third party access effectively without ownership unbundling the supply and transmission assets.[15] The Baltic countries are facing sizeable challenges on their road to achieving a competitive gas sector. The small size of the markets, presence of natural monopolies, long-term contracts with a single supplier and rather ineffective anti-trust authorities discourage the admission other competitors. Due to the lack of physical infrastructure connections with the rest of the EU, Estonia, Latvia and Finland were exempted from the unbundling until 2014. A further solution will be complicated by the fact that Gazprom

---

[15]Iana Dreyer, Fredrik Erixon, and Robert Winkler, "The Quest for Gas Market Competition: Fighting Europe's Dependency on Russian Gas more Effectively," European Centre for International Political Economy, Occasional Paper No. 1, 2010.

essentially controls both supply and distribution businesses in the three Baltic countries.

The new regional, European, as well as global dynamics have, however, already contributed to Russia's partial change of energy interaction with its EU neighbors in the Baltic Sea region. Arguably, Russia has become a more accommodating regional supplier and has attempted to adjust to the transforming markets and trade in the regional and wider European context. The previously held assertive approach has been substituted with more flexible and individually-tailored tactics. Due to the enduring pressures on gas prices Gazprom has apparently been inclined to consider adjusting the existing long-term "take-or-pay" contracts with its Polish and German partners. Some price discounts have been granted to Latvian and Estonian gas companies consecutively in 2011 and 2012. In order to influence regional supply and liberalization dynamics, Gazprom essentially "is gradually moulding a new defensive strategy."[16]

Transatlantic Dimension

The energy security debate in the NATO Riga Summit in 2006 notwithstanding, the transatlantic dimension in the energy security agenda of the Baltic region has been somewhat secondary. The chief transatlantic organization—NATO—primarily focuses on political and military issues and limits its presence in the energy sector to the protection of vital energy infrastructure against military or terrorist attacks. The most pressing energy challenges in the Baltic Sea region—natural gas supplies and liberalization—have been regional and European rather than transatlantic. U.S. involvement has been largely limited to regional energy diplomacy. However, some precursors exist for a more enhanced transatlantic relationship in regional energy security developments. The EU-U.S. Energy Council in 2009 provided an indication of the mutual understanding needed for a stronger institutional interaction between the two transatlantic counterparts. The Council was established to "provide a new framework

---

[16]Anders Aslund, "Gazprom: Challenged Giant in Need of Reform," in Anders Aslund, Sergei Guriev and Andrew Kuchins (eds.), *Russia After the Global Economic Crisis* (Washington, DC: Peterson Institute for International Economics, 2010), p. 162.

for deepening the transatlantic dialogue on strategic energy issues such as security of supply or policies to move towards low carbon energy sources while strengthening the ongoing scientific collaboration on energy technologies."[17] More importantly, some prospective national and regional game changers may contribute to a more intensive involvement of the United States in the energy security dynamics in the Baltic Sea region. This would contribute further to the strengthening of transatlantic links in energy security configuration in the Baltic Sea region.

First, regional interconnections are underway. The EU has facilitated the adoption of the BEMIP. The first steps have already been taken to bring the Baltic countries into the EU energy "mainland" through electricity interconnections, while the next phase would focus more on regional gas market integration. In this regard, further electricity and natural gas interconnections between both Estonia and Finland, and Lithuania and Poland are envisaged. Poland's role is particularly important as the country may serve as both an energy bridge for, and potential natural gas supplier to, the Baltic countries in the future. The interconnections are basically the EU's "homework," yet it would contribute to energy security in the whole transatlantic area.

Second, renewable energy attracts increasing investments and multiplies stakeholders. It promotes cooperation in the region, which has already become the "green energy laboratory" within the EU.[18] The region may essentially become a showcase for further EU and U.S. cooperation in promoting innovation and in setting standards for clean technologies. Moreover, further cooperation on environmental issues and climate change would strengthen a comparative standing of the transatlantic community in the global market of technologies and ideas.[19]

---

[17]EC Press Release, "New EU-US Energy Council to boost transatlantic energy cooperation," 4 November 2009.

[18]Helge Sigurd Næss-Schmidt, "Going for Green Growth in the Baltic Sea Region: Policy Recommendations for Regional Cooperation," Baltic Development Forum Report, 2010.

[19]David Koranyi, *Transatlantic Energy Futures: Strategic Perspectives on Energy Security, Climate Change, and New Technologies in Europe and the United States* (Washington, DC: Center for Transatlantic Relations, 2011).

Third, unconventional resources such as shale gas may become a regional game changer in the medium to longer term. The shale gas revolution in the U.S. has encouraged Poland, as well as Lithuania and Latvia, to pursue domestic natural gas exploration. Although recent projections have discerned less promising reserves of unconventional gas in the region, Poland may still possess considerable potential in developing its own natural gas reserves. Regional production would unequivocally lead to a much more diversified and competitive regional energy market. Latvia and Lithuania have also indicated a strong interest in domestic shale gas exploration. As some observers incisively state: "The closer you get to the Russian border, the more likely it is that shale gas will be made to work."[20] U.S. domestic shale gas developments, U.S. corporate technological and investment capacity, as well as results of environmental studies, particularly in Germany, may influence further developments in the region. Hence, a correlation exists between shale gas exploration in the Baltic Sea region and the strengthening of the transatlantic energy dimension.

Fourth, the region apparently may experience an "LNG race." The first LNG terminal in the region commenced its operation from Nynashamn port, located south of Stockholm in May 2011. In the meantime, alongside the planned Polish (Swinoujscie, 2014) LNG terminal, other countries in the region—Finland, Estonia, Latvia and Lithuania—are considering the construction of their own facilities in the vicinity of their respective capital cities. In March 2012, Lithuania announced that it will lease a Norwegian floating storage and regasification unit from 2014.[21] The LNG developments also reflect a wider tendency that traditionally grid-connected and regionally constrained natural gas supplies are being increasingly transformed into a global commodity trade. This may directly bring the U.S. into the regional configuration. Although the U.S. still needed to import around 100 bcm of natural gas in 2011, the U.S. may become a net exporter in the coming years if the shale gas revolution is sustained. In order to address the lack of liquefaction facilities, which is one of the major obstacles to the country's export agenda, two major export facilities

---

[20]Matthew Hulbert and Karel Beckman, "A quick guide for energy decision-makers: 11 tips, trends and traps for 2012," in *European Energy Review*, 9 January 2012.

[21]Vladimir Socor "Lithuania Contracts for LNG Terminal," *Eurasia Daily Monitor*, 5 March 2012.

are to be developed in the Gulf of Mexico. Cheniere Energy has already signed export contracts with India, South Korea and Spain, and may potentially become a business partner for Germany, Poland, and Lithuania in their efforts to diversify gas supplies and develop regasification facilities.[22]

Fifth, new regional LNG facilities and potential shale gas production would both facilitate natural gas market liberalization attempts by the Baltic countries. In June 2011, as the first member of the European Union to do so, the Lithuanian parliament enacted the respective legislation. It requires ownership seperation of natural gas transmission and distribution infrastructure in the country. The adopted legislation, which should take full effect by 2013, stipulates separating the existing gas transmission and distribution business from Lietuvos Dujos. The adoption of the legislation concurred with the U.S. Secretary of State Hillary Clinton's visit to Lithuania and agreements with U.S. companies to participate in the prospective Lithuanian LNG undertakings (terminal construction and gas supplies).[23] The unbundling, third party access, and new entrants would provide an important window of opportunity for the countries around the Baltic Sea, in general, and Baltic countries in particular, to make the natural gas sector more efficient, price-competitive and make regional markets increasingly integrated, eventually strengthening energy security.

Conclusions

The Baltic energy security architecture remains a work in progress. The structural imbalances and impediments may not be adequately addressed and transformed overnight. Russia largely remains an "indispensable" energy player in the region. However, changing global and regional energy configurations have led to a gradual adjustment of Russia's position in the Baltic Sea region. This has also been facilitated by an increasing EU-ization of the region. A cautious assessment of a common EU voice in security of supply and liberalization notwith-

---

[22]Stratfor, "The United States as Natural Gas Exporter," 12 March 2012.

[23]US State Department, "The United States and Lithuania Strengthen Energy Security Cooperation," Media Note, 1 July 2011; Reuters News, "U.S. Fluor to advise on Lithuania LNG terminal," 1 July 2011.

standing, the region has benefited from a number of community initiatives. As a further step, the new EU External Energy Policy proposal was unveiled in September 2011 with a major goal to ensure coordination and cooperation for the conclusion of intergovernmental agreements in the energy sector.[24] If implemented, this would place bilateral long-term agreements in the Baltic Sea region under a wider European framework. The transatlantic dimension has been less visible in the regional energy security agenda so far. However, a number of common interests exist between partners in the transatlantic energy dialogue. The unconventional gas developments in particular may contribute to the U.S. increasing its engagement in the regional energy developments, especially in the critical and most securitized natural gas sector. And this opens a window of opportunity for the further strengthening of an essential transatlantic dimension in Baltic Sea regional energy security architecture.

---

[24]European Commission, Communication on security of energy supply and international cooperation- "The EU Energy Policy: Engaging with Partners Beyond our Borders," COM (2011) 539, 7 September 2011.

Section V

U.S. Engagement

Chapter Thirteen

Why Does Europe Need the U.S. and the U.S. Need Europe?

Veronika Wand Danielsson

In a rapidly changing globalized world, with the rise of power dynamics in Asia, a strong transatlantic link remains indispensable for enhancing common values and interest within the Euro-Atlantic area and beyond. The U.S. and Europe share the same objectives in promoting democratic governance, the rule of law, open market economies and global trade, while seeking to prevail against corruption and organized crime as they jointly tackle new common security challenges. NATO represents the ultimate embodiment of such strong transatlantic ties through the Euro-Atlantic commitment to the indivisibility of a common security. The United States has for some time now requested a fairer burden-sharing arrangement, in regards to handling of security responsibilities in Europe's periphery if it is to remain engaged in Europe. However, continuous cuts in European and U.S. defense spending, aggravated by the financial crises, are likely to widen the gap between U.S. and European defense capabilities which risks weakening the transatlantic link. Will Robert Gates' "Cassandra warning" materialize the risk that the U.S. will turn its back on Europe unless European allies assume greater strategic responsibilities and invest in the common transatlantic security? Although interests across the Atlantic may diverge from time to time, common values and principles remain the foundation that has tied the transatlantic community together over the last century: The U.S. needs Europe as much as Europe needs the U.S.

Veronika Wand Danielsson is the Swedish Ambassador to NATO.

U.S.-Europe: A Long-Lasting Relationship

The transatlantic relationship has been vital for the stability and security of Europe since World War II. The U.S. engagement in rebuilding Europe after the second devastating European conflict in the 20th century was also instrumental in the development of today's political Europe—as manifested in the European Union (EU). The massive transfer of Marshall Plan funds allowed for the first economic reconstruction efforts in Europe, primarily of Germany. But equally important was the U.S. security presence. The U.S. military presence on European soil had a stabilizing effect that nurtured the slow healing of old antagonism within Germany, as well as between key European countries.

If the initial objective of the U.S. presence was to disarm and demilitarize Germany; the occupational role eventually evolved to that of a protecting power. It was first demonstrated in 1948–1949 during the Soviet blockade of West Berlin. U.S. solidarity with Berlin—as it supplied the city through an Allied airlift, thereby avoiding West Berlin's annexation to the Soviet-zone—changed the overall perception of the U.S. role and presence. The U.S. security presence in Europe was subsequently formalized through the establishment of the North Atlantic Treaty Organisation, NATO, in 1949 and later on the European Security Conference, eventually replaced by the Organization for Security and Cooperation in Europe (OSCE).

NATO formed the security base from which Europe could develop and prosper. It was, for instance, the platform for the restoration of West Germany's sovereignty in May 1955 which, at the same time, required Germany's accession to NATO. And as much as the North Atlantic Alliance became the guarantor of Germany's independence, it represented an overall security shield for Western Europe. Within the Alliance, former enemies became partners.

The Alliance served Europe well during the Cold War as the guarantor of peace and stability in Western Europe. Not surprisingly, after the fall of the Berlin wall in 1989, the newly independent states of Eastern and Central Europe sought NATO membership as their first political objective; to assure their then fragile democracies a lasting security guarantee in turbulent years.

The establishment of Partnership-for-Peace (PfP) in 1994 also allowed for all former satellite states of the Soviet Union to become either members of the Alliance or to be incorporated in the PfP framework. It implied that their ultimate means of power- their armed forces—were integrated into democratic and transparent arrangements. PfP and the Euro-Atlantic Partnership Council, established in 1997, have also been essential cooperation mechanisms for all non-Allied Western European partners, such as Sweden.

Simultaneously, the European Union integration process paved the way for a lasting economic, social and political interdependence in Europe; tying countries so closely together that war, among the members of the European Union, has today become inconceivable.

The Relevance of Transatlantic Security Cooperation Today

The security environment in the Euro-Atlantic area as a whole has seen dramatic changes during the last twenty years. And although most Eastern and Central European countries are tied into the Euro-Atlantic security framework—be it through membership in the Alliance or through the PfP cooperation—there still remain deep, value-based divergences as well as unresolved and frozen conflicts, from the Balkans to the Caucasus and beyond, that merit continuous vigilance. "The little war that shook the world"[1] in Georgia, was only four years ago. Nationalism and ethnic rivalry, often underscored by organized crime, remain worrying features in many parts of the wider Europe, and present a continuous threat to the development of free, open, and democratic societies.

Outstanding security concerns will eventually be resolved through political dialogue and confidence-building measures. However, for the countries and regions concerned, including most Central and Eastern European states, the credibility of the Alliance ultimately lies in its defence of the democratic values of the transatlantic community.

NATO's new Strategic Concept has therefore rightly re-emphasized the fundamental importance of Article V. Strategic reassurance remains important, not only for the Alliance, but also for the stability

---

[1] Ronald Asmus, 2010.

and security of the wider Euro-Atlantic area, including Northern Europe. It is primarily about the U.S. political and military presence in Europe which, through its commitment to the Alliance, remains crucial to the broader European security agenda.

A Swedish Perspective

The relevance of NATO for Allied members, then and today, is true also for non-allied European countries, such as Sweden. Sweden's non-alignment policy, striving for neutrality in wartime, was not a statement against the transatlantic bond. In 1949 it was more about small state "Realpolitik" and very much related to the fragile relationship between Finland and the Soviet Union. An active Swedish participation in the transatlantic defense community could have risked sending Finland down the same road as Czechoslovakia in 1948. During the Cold War the co-operation with Western powers, especially between the U.S. and Sweden, was crucial not least for the Swedish defense capability. The Swedish defence forces were prepared to defend the country against a Soviet invasion should its neutrality policy fail.

Bilateral arrangements and contingency plans existed between Sweden and its Nordic neighbors—NATO members Norway and Denmark—but also, more importantly, with the United States, as revealed in several official reports, academic studies and in a recent book by Swedish journalist Michael Holmström[2]. Sweden's accession to the European Union in 1995 marked a historic shift that placed European solidarity at the center of Sweden's new security policy. Sweden, although militarily non-aligned, has since actively contributed to the development of the European Security and Defence cooperation.

At the same time, the Swedish relationship as a partner with NATO has deepened and expanded. In 2010 the Swedish foreign minister, Carl Bildt, made a clear statement, that the collective defense guarantees in the Washington Treaty—Article V—had played, still plays and

---

[2] *Fred och säkerhet—säkerhetspolitiska utredningen* ("Peace and Security—Security Policy Report") (SOU 2002:108), 2002; Robert Dalsjö, Life-Line Lost—The Rise and Fall of 'Neutral' Sweden's Secret Reserve Option of Wartime Help from the West, 2006; Michael Holmström, *Den dolda alliansen* ("The Hidden Alliance"), 2011.

will continue to play, a crucial role for the security in the Nordic-Baltic area.

Is Europe Really from "Venus"?

With the outbreak of the Iraq War, in 2003, transatlantic relations undoubtedly reached their lowest point. Europe was perceived as coming from "soft power" planet Venus and the U.S. from "hard power" Mars. This misconceived perception would eventually lead to a more ambitious European approach for a common European Security and Defence Policy.

The appointment of a High Representative and the establishment of an External Action Service has helped to focus EU efforts. In crisis management, the EU is working side by side with NATO-led forces in Kosovo and Afghanistan, and U.S.-led units in the fight against piracy around the Horn of Africa. The European Defence Agency is actively contributing to European capability development in close contact with NATO and transatlantic counterparts.

Nevertheless, Americans remain concerned about the European commitment to Europe's own defense agenda. With the financial crises and further budget cuts in Europe, Americans wonder why the U.S. should invest in the defense of Europe, when Europeans do not seem particularly willing to contribute themselves. The farewell speech by Secretary of Defence Robert Gates in July 2011, re-launched the debate about "U.S.-European security cooperation." Europeans should do more, not less. Europe's participation should shoulder more of the Alliance burden, in terms of both its collective defense and its crisis management obligations. Europe should show solidarity and commitment to the common transatlantic agenda. However, Europe should not go its own way.

The Common European Security and Defence Policy remains in the making. A more capable Europe, through a more capable EU, will help rebalance the transatlantic partnership. The European concept of pooling and sharing is about clever investments in a common European defense based on prioritization and closer cooperation at regional, European, and transatlantic levels. The financial crisis forces both sides of the Atlantic to work more effectively together, through the pooling of scarce resources to develop common capabilities. The concept of pooling and sharing in the EU is mirrored by the Smart Defence approach in NATO. With the concept of Smart Defence, NATO's Secretary General, Anders Fogh Rasmussen, has taken decisive steps in this direction. For NATO the challenge is to respond to the Alliance's strategic requirements beyond its three core tasks: collective defense, crisis management, and cooperative security. The participation in common multinational capability projects is not only an issue of burden-sharing or cost effectiveness—important as these may be in a time of financial crises—it is ultimately about tying countries and regions together; it is about political will and about trust in one another.

Rationalizing European procurement and efforts, in order to better integrate military forces and structures across national borders, remains a key European objective. Strong transatlantic relations also require a closer cooperation of the transatlantic defense industry and, ultimately, the development of a genuine transatlantic market for the European and American defense industry. Export controls and barriers impeding cooperation need to be reduced and eventually abolished.

The U.S. as a "Push-Pull" Factor

The concept of national security in the modern world is built on an understanding of solidarity, cooperation and mutual support between nations at national, regional or sub-regional levels. For the Alliance it is built on a strong transatlantic link, both in political and military terms. Most global political and security challenges are today matters of intense consultations and cooperation between the U.S. and its European Allies, including the European Union. There is a clear understanding on both sides of the Atlantic that together the U.S. and Europe can achieve more than either could do so alone. The U.S. engagement in the Balkans or in Georgia remains today the key "push-pull" factor for the Euro-Atlantic integration process of the countries concerned.

In military terms it is about capability and military interoperability. The U.S. plays an essential role in this respect by enhancing military interoperability within the Alliance, and also with NATO's partners.

Interoperability provides for military forces, units, and systems to operate together and to communicate with each other despite different military equipment, systems, and cultures. This has been crucial in the context of international crisis management operations, allowing different armed services to operate coherently together during joint operations. The ISAF-mission with 50 troop-contributing nations operating shoulder to shoulder represents, in this respect, a unique achievement. The push-pull factor of the U.S. military—superior to all Allied nations—should not be underestimated, neither by Allies, nor the partners.

Interoperability is, indeed, in itself a stability promoting objective. For Sweden, as for most other partners, participation in a NATO-led mission is first and foremost about political support and solidarity on an issue of common concern and the readiness to support the implementation of a UN resolution, by participating in the burden-sharing, through a military troop contribution. In 1995, after several years of the UN's challenging peace-keeping mission in the Balkans, NATO entered the scene and, under American leadership, took charge of the first UN-mandated NATO out-of-area operation. The IFOR mission in Bosnia saw a robust Swedish troop contribution which was carried over to SFOR. This was the first Swedish military engagement under the NATO flag. Contributions to NATO-led operations have since continued via KFOR in Kosovo, to ISAF in Afghanistan—which at present is the largest Swedish military commitment in a multinational context.

Further to achieving mutually reinforcing interoperability to a high degree, participation in a crises management operation is, for a troop contributing nation, also a way of gaining valuable experience in return. The more recent NATO-led operation, Unified Protector in Libya, saw a Swedish troop contribution deployed with multi-role fighter-aircraft in a tactical reconnaissance role. The Swedish contribution would not have been possible without Sweden's full interoperability with the Alliance and high readiness, in turn made possible by allowing advanced partners to participate in NATO and U.S.-led exercises and training. Sweden's engagement in NATO-led operations has also helped develop, among other things, our understanding for the necessary "comprehensive approach", the dynamics of counter-insurgency, the challenges of post-conflict management, and the need for close civil-military interaction.

The Libya operation was made possible thanks to the prominent role of European allies and partners in the executive phase of the operation. However, the less-visible U.S. support was absolutely indispensable; in particular in the fields of intelligence and communications. The Libya operation reflected once again the importance of transatlantic cooperation and undoubtedly reinforced the European pillar of the transatlantic link. It proved that Europeans can pull their weight, even in a time of austerity, while sharing the political benefits of a successful mission with the Alliance and its partners. In Libya, the U.S. and European Allies and partners, especially the Arab partners, achieved a common political goal. The Libya mission reflected NATO's new approach to achieving common political objectives, through flexible cooperation and new partnerships. This was significant as not all Allies provided troops. It furthermore proved that a more capable and active Europe is vital for a strong and mutually reinforcing transatlantic link, in the interests of both Europe and the United States.

NATO's well developed partnership policy is indeed one of the Alliance's main strengths and added values, in comparison to many other international organisations. By opening the doors to both regional and global partnerships, not only in the context of troop contribution to NATO-led operations, but also and more importantly, in enabling partners to provide support and active cooperation in common threats and security challenges, NATO is strengthening its overall legitimacy as a global security provider.

The U.S. Needs Europe as Much as Europe Needs the U.S.

The new U.S. Defence Strategy review, through its strategic reorientation towards Asia and the Pacific, is said—by some of Europe's more alarmist voices—to be a direct answer to Robert Gates' "Cassandra warning." It is seen as a clear indication of the U.S.'s fading engagement with Europe.

Adapting the U.S.'s force posture to reflect what was agreed at the Lisbon summit in 2010 on new security challenges of the 21st century, does not necessarily imply "U.S. disengagement." With a continued U.S. commitment to Article V, including more than 70, 000 U.S. military personnel based in Europe; with the deployment of an ambitious missile defense system with military assets in Poland and Romania; a radar in Turkey and Aegis destroyers in Spain; with a deepening cooperation on cyber-security and enhancing the responsiveness of special forces operations; with new training and exercise opportunities for both Allied and partners; and, most importantly also from a European perspective, a strong U.S. focus and presence in the Middle East and North Africa, it seems difficult to claim that the U.S. is turning its back on Europe.

The new U.S. security agenda most certainly serves European interests. And why do I remain optimistic regarding the prospects of the U.S. commitment to Europe? The "best friends" of the United States—those who share its values, its overall policies—both economic and political—are in Europe. There are of course many other friends, present and future, of both the United States and Europe, in other parts of the world. But the transatlantic relationship remains an essential source of stability in an increasingly unpredictable world. Europe has been, and remains, the U.S.'s principle partner in promoting global trade, economic development and security. On most challenges, regional or global, from Kosovo to Georgia, from Afghanistan to Libya, from Iran to the Middle East, European allies and partners work hand in hand with the U.S. In most cases, the U.S. needs European support to achieve national political objectives. In other cases, Europe will need to act alone, and this will also be in the interests of the United States.

The United States needs Europe, as much as Europe needs the United States. This interdependence is presently best reflected through the unique transatlantic solidarity embodied by NATO. The Alliance's new focus on partnerships, which is expected to be highlighted at the Chicago summit, offers further challenging perspectives and opportunities. It is a most welcome development for NATO's partners, including Sweden. With a growing recognition of global security interdependence, Sweden will continue to support and contribute to regional and global security challenges, as a Nordic country, as a committed EU member and as an active partner of NATO.

Chapter Fourteen

U.S.-Nordic-Baltic Engagement in a Globalized World

Ian Brzezinski

At a time when the Euro-Atlantic community struggles to determine how it should address the challenges of the post-Cold War era, more attention should be directed towards the relationship between the United States and the eight democracies of the Nordic-Baltic region. Spanning Demark, Estonia, Finland, Iceland, Latvia, Lithuania, Norway, and Sweden, the Nordic-Baltics are notable for their economic health amidst the ongoing Euro crisis, their readiness to promote democracy beyond their borders, and the laudable contributions they have made to international security and peacekeeping operations. The values and vision that drive their security policies, their demonstrated military capabilities, and their capacity for multinational defense collaboration make them valuable allies and partners of the United States. Further enhancement of the security relationship between the United States and the Nordic-Baltics could yield a new and important pillar in the transatlantic community.

This paper explores how globalization and its economic, political, and security dynamics have increased the relevance of the transatlantic community. It examines the role its Nordic-Baltic dimension can play in managing, deflecting, and leveraging these dynamics. The paper proposes a strategic U.S.-Nordic-Baltic agenda that, if pursued, would serve the security interests of the transatlantic community, reinforce Washington's commitment to it, and increase the prospects of wider East-West political and security cooperation.

Ian Brzezinski served as Deputy Assistant Secretary of Defense for European and NATO Policy from 2001 to 2005. He leads the Brzezinski Group which provides strategic advisory services to US and international companies and he is a Resident Senior Fellow at the Atlantic Council of the United States.

The Global Context of North Atlantic Security:

Today, the transatlantic community lacks consensus over how to address the unprecedented dilemmas inherent in global connectivity and interdependence. Advances in transportation and the ongoing revolution in communications have facilitated the spread of prosperity, respect for human rights and democratic principles of governance among other positive attributes of modernity. However, these benefits have also been accompanied by challenges and changes, including transnational threats, socio-political upheavals, and a decentralization of global power.

Transnational Threats

Among the most urgent of these threats has been the proliferation of technologies pertaining to weapons of mass destruction (WMD), missiles, and other means than can be used to terrorize, if not severely damage, societies. These threats have been accompanied by the emergence of powerful and sometimes dangerous non-state actors, the latter including criminal and terrorist organizations whose ideologies and operations span across continents. The intersection of dangerous non-state actors and WMD today preoccupies much of the attention and concerns of governments.

The Global Political Awakening

The revolution in communications, including global television, the Internet, and cell phones now link previously isolated populations, exposing them not just to each other's economies and cultures, but also to their politics, standards of living, and ideologies. These technologies have not only enhanced the abilities of political activists, they have also empowered individuals with the ability to knowingly or unwittingly stir the emotions of millions. Recent events in Iran, Tunisia, Egypt, Bahrain, and Russia are vivid examples of how this political awakening can bring about change and upheaval.

This dynamic, referred to as a "global political awakening" by Zbigniew Brzezinski (full disclosure—he is my father[1]), is a double-edged

---

[1] Brzezinski, Zbignew, *Strategic Vision: America and the Crisis of Global Power*. Basic Books, 2012. This work also influenced the section on the dispersal of global power.

sword. It can bring down dictators, end corrupt autocracies, and create opportunities for democracy, reform, and accountability in government. It can also be an impatient force, one prone to violence especially when it is driven primarily by sentiments that flow from inequity and injustice. As demonstrated in Russia and the Middle East, this political awakening often generates social upheaval in the absence of leadership, a clear platform or ideology. In these cases, especially if events take a destructive turn, this upheaval can leave societies vulnerable to more organized groups intent on leveraging dangerous ideologies.

The Rise of the Rest and the Dispersal of Power

What some have called the third strategic revolution involves a profound shift in the global balance of power.[2] If 1991 marked a brief unipolar moment featuring a globally preeminent United States, globalization has contributed to the emergence of a more complex constellation of actors with global reach and ambitions. These include China, India, Brazil, Russia, and could well include others in the future.

The implications of these three separate but related dynamics for the transatlantic community are both urgent and profound. Today's world is one where the United States, even in collusion with Europe, is no longer as predominant as it was in the past. The rise of new powers has resulted in a dispersion of global power away from the West and to other regions of world. The fact that meetings of the G-20, which include China, Brazil, and India, are in many ways more significant than those of the G-8 reflects this 21st century redistribution of geo-economic weight. And, with that redistribution a similar dispersion of military capacities becomes likely.

The emergence of new powers with regional, if not global, aspirations is often accompanied by territorial claims, historic grudges, and economic demands that can drive geopolitical tension, competition, and collision. These increase the likelihood of regional conflicts. They make consensual decision-making more difficult, and they yield a world that is more volatile and unpredictable.

---

[2] For insight into the emerging global balance of power and its ramifications see: Brzezinski, Zbigniew, *Strategic Vision* and Zakaria, Fareed, *The Post American World: 2.0*. W.W. Norton & Company, 2011.

Managing this new global order and its proclivity to uncertainty (if not violence) is the defining challenge of our time. Its effective management will require:

- *Economic resources* that can be readily mobilized to foster economic development, if not to stave-off, economic crisis consequent to upheavals;

- *Military capabilities* that are expeditious and can be readily integrated with civilian efforts, including those fostering economic and political development;

- *Ability to tailor engagement and assistance* in keeping with the cultural, historical, and political realities of specific contingencies;

- *Political legitimacy* that is optimized through multilateral versus unilateral action.

It is due to these requirements that the transatlantic community and its key institutions, the North Atlantic Treaty Organization (NATO) and the European Union (EU), have grown in importance. Indeed, due to the growing complexity and turbulence of the post-Cold War era, the democracies of North America and Europe need each other more rather than less. Their respective ability to shape the world order is diluted by divergence and strengthened through collective action.

The transatlantic community brings to the table powerful capacities in each of these four dimensions. Europe and North America constitute the world's most important economic partnership, and that will remain the case for the foreseeable future. Today, the EU and U.S. account for 54% of world gross domestic product (GDP). In 2010, the U.S. generated $15 trillion in GDP, the EU $16 trillion. China in contrast produced $6 trillion in GDP and today lacks partnerships akin to that between the United States and Europe.[3]

Second, the cornerstone of the transatlantic community, NATO, remains history's most successful multinational military alliance. It is unmatched in its ability to generate and sustain interoperability

---

[3] For an insightful annual survey of the EU-US trade relationship, see Daniel Hamilton and Joseph P. Quinlan (eds.), *The Transatlantic Economy 2012*, Center for Transatlantic Relations, John Hopkins University, 2012 (in press).

among military forces, an increasingly challenging requirement in battlefields where operations are ever more technologically complex and whose technologies evolve ever more rapidly. In this regard, the value of NATO has been vividly demonstrated by coalition operations in Afghanistan, Iraq, and most recently Libya in 2011.

Third, members of the transatlantic community, particularly the newest members of NATO and the EU, offer experience useful to societies in North Africa and the Middle East currently on the verge of transitioning from authoritarian to more democratically accountable systems of governance buttressed by market-based economies.

Fourth, the transatlantic community presents a collective of like-minded democracies—and herein lies a vision for its role in the global order of today and tomorrow. It can serve as the core of a geographically and culturally expanding community of democracies that act collectively to promote freedom, stability, and security around the globe.

In a world where power is more dispersed, U.S. and European resources are more constrained, and where international challenges are often best addressed through multilateral approaches, the ability of the transatlantic community to leverage its significant economic heft, its powerful and proven military interoperability, and its democratic legitimacy is invaluable. Only by operating in concert will the nations of Europe and North America be able to tap this potential in the effort to manage the complex volatility consequent to the urgent and lethal threats posed by transnational threats, social upheavals, and rising new powers.

The Nordic Baltic Dimension

The Nordic-Baltic region constitutes a distinctive and important dimension of the transatlantic community. When viewed as a region, these countries represent a population of 32 million and a gross national product approaching $1.5 trillion.[4] They include both the

---

[4] For an outstanding description of the tangible and political attributes the Nordic-Baltic region brings to the transatlantic community, see: Damon Wilson and Magnus Nordeman, "The Nordic-Baltic Region as a Global Partner of the United States" in *Nordic-Baltic Security in the 21ˢᵗ Century*, Altantic Council, 2011.

most developed countries in the world as well as those that have most successively transitioned from the authoritarianism and command economy of the Soviet Union.

As a community, the Nordic-Baltics embody the powerful assets the transatlantic community can bring to bear. Moreover, the region is distinguished by four assets that should compel U.S. policy-makers to recognize it as a valuable element of the transatlantic community. They are: Values, Vision, Capability and Collaboration.

Values

The Nordic-Baltics are leaders in the effort to promote democracy, rule of law, human rights, and market-based development in Europe and around the world. Their efforts are advantaged by the absence of colonial and great power legacies that often complicate the engagements of the U.S. and other European countries in Africa, Asia, the Middle East, and elsewhere around the globe. Of all the nations that constitute the transatlantic community, they are mostly regarded as "honest brokers" in the world's hotspots.

Vision

The Nordic-Baltics, including neutral Sweden and Finland, have been steadfastly committed to the vision of a Europe whole, free, undivided, and secure. Within the region one finds countries that are second to none in supporting the aspirations of those in Ukraine and Georgia who envision their countries as future members of NATO and the European Union.

Capability

While the Nordic-Baltic region consists of medium-sized states and small states, they together offer significant useable, deployable military assets. These include nearly 300 combat aircraft, 110,000 active duty military personnel, and a variety of maritime assets.[5] They are experienced in multinational peacekeeping operations under the flags of the

---

[5] Damon Wilson and Magnus Nordeman, "The Nordic-Baltic Region as a Global Partner of the United States" in *Nordic-Baltic Security in the 21ˢᵗ Century*, Altantic Council, 2011.

EU, the United Nations (UN), and NATO. Sweden recently contributed its Gripen aircraft and Demark and Norway contributed F-16s to the NATO mission over Libya in 2011, and every country in the region has contributed in some way to the Alliance's effort in Afghanistan.

Collaboration

The Nordic-Baltics present a cohesive group of democracies that have long shed national rivalries and who present outstanding models of multinational military cooperation. Despite the region featuring overlapping NATO and EU memberships, defense collaboration is far reaching. Nordic Defense Cooperation (NORDEFCO) encompasses each of the Nordic states and recently established a relationship with the three Baltics states. It promotes joint training and exercises, joint procurement, and joint operations to maximize the military capacities of these countries. This platform now includes the establishment of NORDEFCO Task Force, common ground air defense procurement programs, and multi-national logistics systems. NATO operations in Afghanistan have benefited from NORDEFCO initiatives and the initiative has supported the capacity development of the Eastern Africa Stand-By Forces.

A U.S.-Nordic-Baltic Action Security Agenda for the 21st Century

The values, vision, capabilities, and collaboration the Nordic-Baltics bring to the transatlantic table make them a compelling partner for the United States. A U.S.-Nordic-Baltic agenda can leverage these attributes to address regional and global developments affecting the transatlantic community. That agenda could include the following elements:

1. Revitalized Vision of a Europe Whole, Free, and Secure

The U.S. and the Nordic-Baltic States should leverage their shared political weight to reanimate as a guiding priority of the transatlantic community the vision of a Europe whole, free, and secure. This vision has lacked enthusiastic endorsement and action from President Obama and many Western European governments.

Revitalizing the vision of a Europe whole, free and, secure would contribute to a more effective strategy supporting Russia's evolution toward democracy as well as towards being a more constructive international actor. Its fulfillment would preclude a new zone of insecurity that would only distance Russia from the rest of Europe and sustain the influence of those in Moscow still burdened with nostalgic inclinations to recreate a Russian sphere of influence.

In the absence of an energized vision of a completed Europe, transatlantic security policy has denied itself an important forward-driving objective. Its reanimation would provide a focus and purpose that can renew institutional life and energy to the community's engagement with those European countries that remain outside of NATO and the EU.

This point is relevant to the Enhanced Partnership in Northern Europe (ePINE) program involving the U.S. and Nordic-Baltic states. Among its initiatives, ePINE has promoted human rights, market reform, and democratic practices of governance in states of the former Soviet Union. Without the goal of an undivided Europe to drive it forward, ePINE is at risk of devolving into a mission-less consultative mechanism rather than the vision-driven force it once was.

The vision of Europe whole and free served that purpose in the 1990s and much of the first decade of this century. The fact that this vision remains unfulfilled and because it serves the common values of freedom and security means that its utility and power is far from diminished.

2. Arctic Security

The growing accessibility of the Arctic facilitated by new technologies and the steady reduction of the polar ice cap will in the coming decades directly affect the interests of the U.S. and the Nordic-Baltic states. The Arctic is a region rich in oil gas, nickel, iron ore, and rare earth minerals, and will likely emerge as an important transportation route, particularly between Europe and Asia. Already, Russia and China have taken steps toward increasing their presence in this area. As countries and companies seek to leverage these economic potentials, they will generate a challenging set of resource management, environmental, sovereignty, border security, and related geopolitical issues.

How to address these issues in a common coordinated fashion should become a focus of U.S.-Nordic-Baltic cooperation. A common approach can usefully influence deliberations on these issues within the United Nations, the European Union, NATO, the Arctic Council, and other multinational fora.

3. Coordinated Engagement of Russia

The Nordic-Baltic region shares a common border with Russia as well as interests in the Arctic and the Baltic Seas. The region has unique historical experience and diplomatic skill in understanding Russia and dealing constructively with its leadership. In addition to pressing forward the vision of a Europe whole and free, the United States and the Nordic-Baltics should leverage their capacities in ways to deepen their engagement with the Russian society and state. In this regard, ePINE could serve as a platform for joint U.S.-Nordic-Baltic engagement with Russia.

In the realm of security cooperation, consideration should be given on how to engage both the United States and Russia in military exercises and other confidence building activities conducted under the auspices of NORDEFCO. Shared concerns in the Baltic Sea could serve as a preliminary focus of such efforts. In a similar manner, engaging Russia in U.S.-Nordic-Baltic initiatives concerning mutual interests in the Arctic, such as maritime safety, could be another means to ensure that the region does not devolve into unhelpful, if not antagonistic, rivalry.

4. Leverage Nordic-Baltic Capacities for Out-of-Area Operations

The Nordic-Baltic countries offer some of the world's best expertise in maritime operations, especially littoral security and warfare. They offer capable coastal patrol boats, minesweepers, submarines, and oceangoing combatants, all of which are relevant to the challenges and crises present in today's maritime commons (indeed, Swedish submarines have often outwitted both U.S. and European forces in naval exercises.) These capacities should be leveraged to support international coalitions operating outside of the North Atlantic Area.

Offering such capacities to support U.S.-led operations patrolling the Persian Gulf and the Strait of Hormuz would demonstrate transatlantic solidarity in the face of Iranian threats to disrupt shipping in these waterways. It would be fully consistent with the contributions Denmark and Norway have made to NATO's anti-piracy operation off the Horn of Africa, Ocean Shield, and those made by Denmark, Estonia, Lithuania, Finland, and Sweden to the EU's anti-piracy mission in that region. A Nordic-Baltic contribution to the U.S.-led task force in the Persian Gulf would resonate well in the United States, where many question Europe's commitment to stand with Washington in out-of-area contingencies.

5. Deepening U.S.-Nordic-Baltic Military Engagement

In January 2012, following the release of its new Defense Policy Guidance, the Obama Administration announced its decision to reduce the U.S. military presence in Europe. To help make up for that reduction, Washington promised rotations of U.S.-based forces to Europe to participate multinational and NATO-led training and exercises. These rotations should be structured so as to maximize U.S.-Nordic-Baltic military engagements, including the use of the region's training facilities.

In addition to hosting U.S. forces, the Nordic-Baltic countries should also offer to rotate elements of their own forces—for example, the Nordic Battlegroup—to exercises conducted in North America. By making the trip across the Atlantic the Nordic-Baltics would leverage state of the art training facilities in the United States and would enhance and underscore their readiness to undertake expeditionary operations.

Consideration should be given to engaging the United States in NORDEFCO multilateral capability development efforts, including the procurement of weapons platforms and enablers and military research and development. The EU and NATO promote military multinational pooling and sharing initiatives, but both tend to yield largely European initiatives involving little U.S. input. U.S.-NORDE-FCO initiatives would fit well within NATO's Smart Defense initiatives and inject it with a needed dose of transatlanticism.

6. Nordic-Baltic Contributions to the NATO Response Force (NRF)

A number of the region's militaries have contributed to NRF rotations on a national basis. As NATO moves to revitalize the NRF, the U.S. has promised to permanently commit a U.S. battalion to the force. The Nordic-Baltic region could complement this U.S. contribution by assigning their regional units, such as the Nordic Battlegroup, to NRF rotations. The experience of NRF rotations, particularly with a U.S. ground element assigned to the force, would be another useful means of developing and sustaining expertise in expeditionary operations. It would also provide another means of fostering sustained engagement among U.S. and Nordic-Baltic militaries.

U.S.-Nordic-Baltic cooperation can serve as an important new pillar of the transatlantic community. The vision, values, capabilities, and collaboration that define the Nordic-Baltics make them a valuable partner for the United States. This transatlantic pillar can be used to reanimate the effort to build a wider and more secure Europe and to deepen cooperation with Russia. U.S.-Nordic-Baltic collaboration can also reinforce America's commitment to Europe's regional security requirements and simultaneously drive forward the transatlantic community's effort to address the global challenges defining this new century.